THE
DEMCRACY
OF
WAR

ANSTRUTHER AND CELLARDYKE
IN THE FIRST WORLD WAR

KEVIN DUNION

Kevin Dunion studied history at St. Andrews University. He worked on international development and the environment before becoming the Scottish Information Commissioner. He is author of two previous books, Living in the Real World - The International Role for Scotland's Parliament (1993) and Troublemakers - the Struggle for Environmental Justice in Scotland (2003). He lives in Cellardyke.

THE DEMOCRACY OF WAR

ANSTRUTHER AND CELLARDYKE IN THE FIRST WORLD WAR

KEVIN DUNION

KILRENNY AND ANSTRUTHER BURGH COLLECTION

The Democracy of War

Anstruther and Cellardyke in the First World War

Published by the Kilrenny and Anstruther Burgh Collection.
39B John Street, Cellardyke, KY10 3BA

www.democracyofwar.co.uk

ISBN 978-0-9536538-4-3

Illustrations

Contents

Foreword

The Fife fishing communities of Anstruther and Cellardyke have always asserted their separate identities, and not even the upheaval of the First World War could change that, which is why two war memorials flank the communities, like two monumental bookends.

Who are the 102 men (and one woman) commemorated on them? None of them are famous; none achieved high rank (none are above the rank of captain). Some are decorated but there are no VCs amongst them. None has left us any war poetry. None even appear as bit players in the increasingly inclusive histories of the First World War which draw upon the testimony of ordinary soldiers.

What did the loss of these ordinary, barely-remembered people mean to the community and to those left behind? When the celebrated writer Vera Brittain wrote to her fiancé about the death of Rudyard Kipling's son she said she always felt sorrier when those killed are the sons of intellectual and brilliant people. "I don't know how it should be, but somehow I always feel that they must mean even more to their parents than those of the more ordinary ones do to theirs."[1]

Even as a front line soldier he seemed to share this sense of differential worth. He wrote a letter to Vera saying that there was a grave a few yards away from where he was sitting. It was the grave of a private soldier. Nearby there was the grave of a major around which he had put a new fence. "I cannot help thinking of the two together and of the greater value of the one." he wrote. "What a pity it is that the same little piece of lead takes away as easily a brilliant life and one that is merely vegetation. The democracy of war!..." [2]

This may be the view of those who shared that unattractive combination of the arrogance of youth and the insensitive carapace of class. But for millions of others these notions would offend. Britain is studded with war memorials which attest to a shared national sense that the democracy of war means that the choice of who is honoured should not depend upon military status, the nature of wartime service or the manner of death. Waves closed over regular sailors on battleships as well as reservists on converted fishing boats. Professional soldiers fought alongside enthusiastic volunteers and conscripts doing their duty. They

---

[1] Bishop and Bostridge p173
[2] ibid p111

1

died fighting; they were shelled, sniped, mined in trenches; they expired from wounds; they succumbed to illness. All were to be judged worthy of commemoration.

The names on the Anstruther and Cellardyke memorials are of those ordinary people who were regarded as having done something extraordinary. Nobody is quite sure how many Scots died in the First World War but including those who died in the colonial forces it is thought to be 148,000. In that case these local memorials account for only 0.07% of the Scottish war dead. Yet the war can be traced through their experience. They died when Britain lost its first naval battle for 100 years. They drowned at Jutland, the biggest naval encounter in naval history. They fell at Loos, suffered privations in Gallipoli. They were slaughtered on the first day of the Somme when more men were lost than on any single day in military history; they perished at Arras and Passchendaele. They took on von Richthofen in the skies above the trenches and lost. They drew upon centuries of maritime experience, and steamed off in their own fishing boats to search out submarines and sweep away mines and were sunk by them both. They exposed themselves to mortal danger and at times were put in the way of certain death. They left behind families who were proud and those who were bitter.

For us they remain in history's sepia tones, captured in the mind's eye as grainy figures disjointedly marching and falling. Their connection with us is severed by time and all that has taken place since then. But for anybody living in Anstruther and Cellardyke, their names are familiar as their families are still prominent. By pulling together what information can be gleaned, a more rounded picture of what these men and women experienced and contributed can be appreciated.

I am grateful for the help of many local people in assisting with this project. Jim Tribble, Murray Anderson, Masry Prince, Keith Otto, Glenn Jones, John Barker and Pam Cranston of the Kilrenny and Anstruther Burgh Collection read drafts, sourced financial support and suggested local contacts. Iain Duncan, Rector of Waid Academy acted as referee for our application to the Heritage Lottery Fund. Photographs, medals, old letters of relatives were brought down from attics in response to my request for help. I am particularly grateful to Sandy Watson and his wife Doris who entrusted me with the letters and documents of Willie Watson and who so enthusiastically responded to my inquiries about him and the family. I am also indebted to Christine Keay for providing me with the information about her grandfather Alex Doig; to John Smith for information on Tom Smith and for tracking down the rare photographs of him and to David Brown and John Brown for letting me know about the remarkable military career of their forebear who joined up in 1899 and fought through the Boer War, First World War and finally Afghanistan before returning to Cellardyke. (Tragically David was drowned last year when his boat capsized when putting out his lobster creels just off the rocks at Cellardyke.) Alexander (Sonny) Corstorphine supplied details about his uncle Alexander Corstorphine as well as for George Corstorphine and John Bett. Norma Brown did sterling service tracking down the attestation papers of all those on the memorials who served with the Canadian forces. Alan Watson supplied details of his prisoner-of-war grandfather, George Watson. Dr Stephanie Stevenson gave me fascinating details about the Darsie family as well as the photographs of George Darsie. Mrs Betty Peebles entrusted me with the only photograph of her father, Skipper John Hughes, in uniform.

Thomas Smyth, Archivist in the Black Watch Museum, Perth helpfully pointed me in the right direction in response to early inquiries. The staff and volunteers at the Scottish Fisheries Museum drew on their extensive archives to find relevant photographs of boats and local seaman, several of which are reproduced with their permission. So too the staff at the Special Collections Department, University of St Andrews recovered photographs from the old local papers.

I am very grateful to the Heritage Lottery Fund for providing financial support to bring this project to fruition.

Above all, my wife Linda has encouraged me in the happy belief that the countless hours spent in libraries, museums and in correspondence were well spent.

Finally, I am well aware that there will be many memories, photographs, and sources which have still to be brought to light. This book does not bring about the end of our research but marks only where we have come so far. More information, comments, links and enquiries are welcome through our website **www.democracyofwar.org.uk** to which new material will be added.

Kevin Dunion
Cellardyke 2007

Chapter 1

Anstruther and Cellardyke
on the eve of the First World War

Nowadays you might be forgiven for believing, wrongly, that the houses and churches, school and shops which fan out around Anstruther harbour, hugging the coastline east and west and occupying fertile land to the north, form a single community. Back in 1914 people would be less understanding of such a misapprehension, and you certainly would not want to make the mistake in the presence of John Porter, the irascible and indomitable Provost of Anstruther Wester. He was incensed at the proposals coming from the leaders of the neighbouring burghs of Anstruther Easter and Kilrenny that they should set aside local rivalries in favour of municipal amalgamation. Provost Porter was having none of it. Anstruther Wester was a Royal Burgh in its own right. He feared that the amalgamation would allow the other burghs to plunder his Common Good Fund and to raise the rates to help pay for harbour improvements. The local newspaper the *Coast Burghs Observer* devoted pages to the fraught negotiations. Tempers ran high. Provost Porter claimed to have been petitioned by every businessman and property owner in the burgh against amalgamation. Not so said colleagues from his own Council, some of whom actually favoured combining with their neighbours, and who denounced their leader as autocratic.

This was but yet the latest manifestation of a proposal going back decades. Anstruther could trace its history back to the 12th century when the first written account of it indicates that a thriving fishing trade was already well established around the natural haven at the mouth of the Dreel Burn. It received its Royal Charter in 1587, confirming its freedom from Pittenweem. Anstruther Easter, across the burn, had also secured its separation from Kilrenny by the same process and had a more substantial harbour which could accept larger ships but which over the following centuries would need constant repair and expansion, draining local revenues. The Burgh of Kilrenny even further east was dominated by the settlement of Cellardyke, which too had its own harbour, and was almost entirely given over to fishing and its associated trades, whilst Kilrenny village itself was set apart from the shorefront communities, serving the farming hinterland. All three burghs fiercely preserved their own identities. When the construction of reservoirs to supply clean drinking water became a national crusade, Anstruther Wester made plans for its own supply, refusing at first to consider joining with Anstruther Easter and Cellardyke.[3] There had been previous attempts at amalgamation in the early 19th century but these were howled down, although a measure of co-operation and common purpose was recognised with the construction of the Union harbour at Anstruther Easter (built by Thomas Stevenson, father of Robert Louis who came to live in Anstruther in 1868). Further pragmatic mergers did take place. The population of Anstruther Easter was only 1147 and that of Wester only 631, yet both maintained separate school boards. In July 1913 notice was given that these would amalgamate. Whilst some saw this as the precursor to ever closer municipal merger, such ideas still inflamed hostile resistance. So it was at the outbreak of war each community still had its own structures of town councils, provosts and baillies, parish churches and town halls.

There was no shortage of men to take on civic roles. Public service was a sought after duty for professionals and business men in the burghs. Even school board elections would attract more nominations than places available (although, conveniently, subsequent withdrawals would mean that ballots were often not required). In 1914 the Anstruther School Board elections list was headed by William Scott Bonthron, a fish curer, and he was joined on the list by an engineer, a manufacturer, banker, a minister, two solicitors and a law clerk. Cellardyke School Board included kenspeckle figures like John Thomson, a draper, and the Rev James Ray, the energetic and well respected minister. Amongst 3 farmers putting their names forward for the school board election was David Clements from Easter Pitkerie, farming out of town on the St Andrews Road, with the other places being contested by a baker, a manufacturer and 2 merchants.

Such men had prominence in local public, business and social life. Baillie Alex Burd was a thriving local watchmaker and jeweller whose adverts for wedding rings, gold bracelets and spectacles and "eyeglasses to suit all sights from 2/- per pair" graced the front pages of the local newspaper weekly. There was more to life than work and local politics for Baillie Burd as he was a stalwart of the local golf club and with his friend Provost Porter ensured that Anstruther Wester Town Council regularly preoccupied itself over how to extend and improve the little course at the Billowness between Anstruther and Pittenweem.

---

[3] Smout p102

Waid Academy 1905
Elizabeth Johnston (middle row second from left) would die while serving
with Queen Mary's Army Auxiliary Corps in France.

Certainly the great and the good of Anstruther lived active social lives. Provost Oliphant of neighbouring Anstruther Easter might have a demanding job as a banker but could be found with his Town Clerk, the prominent local solicitor Charles Maxwell, enjoying a game of whist in local tournaments. Cllr GM Black, baker and Honorary Treasurer of the Cellardyke Town Council enjoyed his game of bowls with the local bowling club; whilst David Cook solicitor and member of Anstruther School Board was a formidable partner with his wife at the tennis club.

Amongst the foremost local families were the Darsies. The family is said to be able to trace its lineage back to the Norman conquest, and is recorded as being in Anstruther from the mid 16th century. Darsies held prominent roles as councillors, baillies and magistrates for generations, but they were hardworking, hard-nosed men of trade, variously being shipmasters, fishcurers, and tanners. A sense of the exotic was introduced when George Darsie married a Tahitian princess Titaua Marama. In 1856 at 14 she had been married to John Brander a wealthy English trader, whom she bore 9 children. After Brander's death she married her manager George Darsie in 1878, and she bore him 3 children, Georgina, George and Lieumonte. He brought her back to Anstruther and their substantial house, Johnston Lodge in Hadfoot Wynd hosted guests such as a beautiful young Hawaian princess.[4]

Georgina and George Darsie (standing at back)-
their mother was a Tahitian princess. He was killed in France, 1918.

The impression of stolid stability is reinforced by the physical presence of these men. Their homes were often substantial and their addresses were so well known as not to require street name or numbers - they could be found simply by their house name such as 'Craigholm', or 'Clifton'. The prominence of this presence found its way into local usage. David Cook's house was used, for instance, by local fishermen for navigation purposes. When boats were out in the Forth and trying to establish their position or return to a favourite fishing ground they would line up two prominent landmarks as a fix. These were called 'meids' - old Scots for mark or measurement. For instance "Kellie ower Hughies" would see Kellie Law lined up with what is now the Craw's Nest Hotel but which used to be the manse of Anstruther Wester Kirk and was occupied by Rev Hew Scott. So another meid was "Kellie ower Cook's hoose" - Kellie Law lined up with 'High Cross', David Cook's house.[5]

These people had a place society even if that society was confined to

---

[4] Stevenson pp.199-200

[5] Watson p233

the citizenry of the three burghs. The Philharmonic dance in the Town hall in April 1914, we are told, was graced by Mrs WS Bonthron (the fish curer's wife) in a dress of old gold satin charmeuse; Mrs Burd (the jeweller's wife) in a tango satin dress with a bodice of shadow lace; Mrs Cook (the solicitor's wife) in cream silk crepon; and Mrs Maxwell (the Town Clerk's wife) resplendent in a brown silk crepe with cherie sash.

Waid Academy 1906. Robert Ray (front row, second from left) went on to become a government scientist, developing explosives during the war.

Their children too were also given public recognition (if they were successful that is). Robert Ray the son of the Cellardyke Minister was building a strong academic career having graduated with double honours from St Andrews University and thereafter being awarded a Carnegie scholarship to carry out research in north west England, before heading off in 1913 to be Lecturer in Zoology at the University of South Africa in Cape Town.

His younger brother Philip had gone from the Waid Academy to study for a B.Sc. in engineering at Glasgow University, and his progress was proudly reported in the local press (we are told with precision that he came 7th (equal) in his first year). The scholastic achievements of his younger contemporaries at Waid Academy were also faithfully recorded.

In August 1914 passes in the Leaving certificate exams were noted for John Smith Parker, Andrew Dick, John Smith and Thomas Smith. Rare recognition for some was provided by the publication of a photograph of the Waid Senior Boys Hockey team in June 1914 (photographs being uncommon in the local press) and we can see the Tom Brown's schooldays image of strapping young men - J Parker, baby faced R Elder, W Bonthron and blonde-haired Tom Smith with a bandage around a gashed left knee.

Beyond this group the individual folk of Anstruther and Cellardyke are largely anonymous to the outside world. A hardworking and bustling community, the wages from fishing, farming, oilskin manufacturing and golf club making were spent at Gray and Pringles sales, or by going to the pictures at the weekend in the Town Hall. Local excitement would be generated by the arrival of attractions such as Bostock and Wombwells menagerie which boasted the only travelling hippopotamus, Bengal tiger, Snow Leopard and tasmanian devil. Sporting rivalries were fostered, none more so than through the local football team Anster Rangers which cleared the decks with rivals Leven Celtic 4-0 in April 1914.

However it took tales of tragedy, injury, great coincidence and good deeds or wrong-doing to bring forward individuals from the throng. Harry Bowman (18) apprentice painter with D Walker and Sons monosyllabically endured being cross examined at a fatal accident inquiry at Cupar Sheriff Court which found that the collapse of scaffolding at the town hall which killed a work mate was an accident. Miss Bissett, working in a field at Milton Farm, found a wedding ring belonging to her companion Mrs Anderson which had been lost five years previously, when working in the same field. David Thomson, cleek finisher, was fined 2s 6d with the option of spending 3 days in prison for breaking two bottles and throwing glass in the street. Baillie Burd sentencing him said magistrates were determined to put down this practice and any future offences would be more severely dealt with.

Fishermen come drifting out of the ranks. When in August 1914, ten year old John Thomson fell off the Middle pier and was in danger of drowning "a fisherman named Bett from Fowler Street in Cellardyke went down the ladder and had him fished out". Earlier in the month it was reported that a Cellardyke youth John Bett had dived into the harbour to save young Alex Ritchie who had fallen in. Sometimes fisherman were in need of assistance themselves - David Smith came to grief at the sharp corner at Buckie House when cycling down the High Street and ran full tilt into two farm carts full of potatoes. After medical attention he was returned to his home in Pittenweem by train. However real tragedy was never far away for fishing communities and even before the war young lives were cut short. John Wilson of James Street, Cellardyke was lost after being washed overboard from the drifter *Baden Powell*, the rest of the crew coming north by train from Shields with the sad news.

Whilst public office provided prominence for leading lights there was still the expectation that others would do their bit for the greater good. The Territorial Army provided the opportunity for fit young men but there was concern that perhaps the sense of duty was not being fostered in this younger generation. When the local complement of Territorials mustered under Lieutenant Maxwell (solicitor, town clerk etc.) for their annual church parade at the beginning of June 1914, Rev James Ray was concerned at the apparent reluctance of young men to join the ranks. "He fervently hoped it did not mean that the youth of the country were less patriotic than their fathers or that they were indifferent to the fate of their native land." He believed that "were immediate danger apprehended they would rise willingly and promptly" but he asked "might it not be too late to do so then? With the enemy at our gates what use would be an army, however large, of untrained and undisciplined men."

It would be easy to read into his words some prescience of what was to come. The impression has been given by some that the war was recognised as being almost inevitable given the armaments race embarked upon by Germany - and that Germany was the obvious enemy which Rev Ray would have in mind. Popular novels and plays drew upon rumours of German spies and fears of invasion.

But for the Rev Ray, the threat of war even in June 1914 still seemed remote. His concern was not that Britain was unready for what appeared to be imminent conflict. Rather the opposite - it was the lack of any apparent immediate threat to our shores which meant that the young men of Anstruther felt they had better things to do with their time than join the Territorials. The people of Anstruther and Cellardyke were little different from many others in going about their business believing that the twentieth century had ushered in a period of rapprochement amongst the superpowers. This was not borne out of naivety of the realpolitik of superpower manoeuvrings. Even modern day historians have concluded "The evidence is unequivocal: Europeans were not marching to war, but turning their backs on militarism".[6] War close to home seemed an unlikely prospect, a view echoed by the Reverend Ray who, after bemoaning the theoretical danger that lack of patriotic duty presented, consoled himself and his congregation with the confident thought that "the lust for war was dying out in the civilised world and our statesmen shrank as never before from doing anything that would break the peace."

Less than 10 weeks later Britain would be embroiled in a war which would shatter his family and the lives of many in his congregation.

[6] Ferguson p30

Chapter 2

Answering the call to arms

War had an immediate effect upon Anstruther. In the first week of August 1914 the banks did not open, staple goods doubled in price in local shops and worse was expected. "It is understood that the cooper yards and oilskin manufacturers in Anstruther will be closed down at the end of this week and in this way an exceptionally large number of women and girls will be thrown out of employment" reported the *Coast Burghs Observer* which feared what the future may hold - "It is most distressing to even imagine what the results of all this will be."

In these first weeks the attitudes to war were ambivalent. It has been often suggested that the reported extent of the enemy losses encouraged young men to sign up, anxious not to miss out on what might be a short lived but certainly victorious war. In mid August the future Field Marshall, but at that time lowly Lieutenant, Bernard Montgomery predicted "at least the thing will be all over in three weeks."[7] However it is worth noting that, locally at least, German deaths on such a scale did not occasion triumphalism in the local press but instead fostered a notion of dread. The early hostile engagements brought immediate recognition of the scale of losses which might lie ahead and that once embarked on all out conflict it would be difficult to escape without paying a high price. Before it was fully swept up in the patriotic enthusiasm of recruitment the local paper had one last agonised call to reason. Reporting that up to 60,000 casualties were suffered by German troops in the fighting at the end of August, it lamented "that this frightful slaughter should have to go on is a terrible thought. Is there no way of bringing the war to an end before all the parties are completely exhausted by such a bloody struggle?"

Whilst the Germans were indeed suffering substantial losses, Allied propagandists have been accused of inflating the German casualty figures. Claims had been made of 25,000 Germans being killed and wounded in one assault when in fact the Germans had 18,000 officers and men killed in the whole of August across the entire Western Front. By contrast it was France which was suffering frightful slaughter with 100,000 killed and missing in the August fighting.

However in Anstruther gloomy reflection was soon displaced by stirring

---

[7] Vansittart p.30

anecdotes of recruiting fever. "Hurry up Captain I want to be taken on at once and get at 'em" was how Captain Steven the local Recruiting Officer claimed to be assailed, in what sound suspiciously unlike East Neuk tones. Patriotic parents queued up to give away their sons "I'm too old myself but you can have my two sons" whilst another came bearing a note from his mother which said " Sir, the bearer of this letter is over 19 years of age, make a soldier of him."

The call to arms was responded to most immediately by men who had been prepared to defend the country but had not expected to go abroad to do so. The Territorial army had been established in 1908 as a result of army reforms which had been prompted precisely because of the perceived threat coming from Germany. By 1910 over a quarter of a million men had joined up.[8]

By the time of war however the Territorials were not held in high esteem. The training was felt to be inadequate. In 1910 over one third of the Force failed to pass the musketry test. In 1912 only 155,000 out of 252,000 NCOs and men attended camp.[9] The problem was of course getting time off. Some men could not afford to take time away from work or their employer refused them leave. It was only in 1914 that a bounty of £1 was agreed to be paid to men who completed the full fifteen days camp.

The men of the East Neuk joined the Black Watch 7th Battalion. According to the Battalion's Diary and Almanac officers and men had to undergo 40 drills in the first year of their recruitment, attend annual training camp and take part in a musketry course. To qualify for allowances at least 20 drills had to be completed before going to camp. Locally at least it seems the Territorials were in good order. Captain Murray and Lieutenant Maxwell were imposing local figures who had been involved with the Volunteer Battalion and simply carried on after reorganisation with the Territorials. The annual visit to the firing range at Kincraig in July 1913 saw the men perform well despite the "boisterous weather", and promotions to Lance Corporal were made to C. Easton, W. Watson and W. Elliot.[10]

Yet the Territorials were clearly second class soldiers and were made to feel so even down to the degree to which they were allowed to identify

---

[8] Middlebrook p.4

[9] Dennis p.26

[10] EoFR 3 July 1913

with their parent regiment. One of the drills for the local men was the annual church parade. Lieutenant Maxwell placed an advert notifying the men to muster at the Drill hall and specifying the wearing of "Red Tunics, Trews, Spats, Glengarry with Waistbelt and Side Arms." For a kilted regiment to appear on a formal occasion with trews seems odd, but it appears that the local Black Watch Territorials actually had no kilts.[11] In November 1913 at a meeting of the Fifeshire Territorials Sir Ralph Anstruther, Colonel Commanding the 7th Royal Highlanders sought to remedy this by proposing a motion that the kilt should be adopted. However this was opposed by Colonel Mitchell, the Officer Commanding the Fife and Forfar Yeomanry, on the grounds that it would cost £2500 to do so. The dispute went to the casting vote of Lord Elgin who chaired the meeting and he turned down the proposal.[12]

The local detachment in Anstruther reportedly comprised 41 men, all but two of whom responded to the call to muster at the Drill Hall on 5 August. The local men in their uniforms and with their guns attracted excited attention. A crowd surrounded a group of Territorials on Shore Street, where an over-inquisitive admirer pulled the trigger of a rifle. A bullet whistled through the crowd, hitting nobody before lodging in the upper storey of the house next to the Murray Library. The local paper thought this was highly reprehensible and called for the Territorial to be punished for irresponsibly carrying a loaded weapon in a crowd of people.[13]

Instead within days the culprit was off to war - or at least off to Kinghorn along the coast to prepare for war. In scenes which were no doubt being repeated around the country the men "fully equipped and bronzed with their recent camp experience filed out of the hall in marching order about 7 o'clock. They were accorded an enthusiastic send off from the large concourse of townspeople... the route being lined with people of all ages and classes ringing cheers being raised and handkerchiefs waved on all sides."[14]

Whatever the intent of politicians, the local Territorials were not men who had joined up in the expectation of going to fight the Germans - far from it. Territorials could not be sent abroad even at a time of war without

---

[11] Yet this does not seem to be the case for other Black Watch Territorials. The 5th Black Watch passed through Crieff on a route march in July 1914, and the men were photographed by a local cameraman. The picture shows the men in shirtsleeves but with their kilts and sporrans.

[12] EoFR 13 November 1913

[13] EoFR 14 August 1914

[14] CBO 13 August 1914

signing an Imperial Service Obligation. This was a major impediment to the notion of the Territorials supporting Regulars in any expeditionary force. In 1913 only 1,152 officers and 18,903 NCO's and men had voluntarily taken the Imperial Service Obligation.[15] Even with the outbreak of war not all of the local detachment signed up to go. Clearly this was a matter of some sensitivity. When the local Territorials marched off, the *Coast Burghs Observer* not unnaturally wanted to acknowledge the first of Anstruther's sons to do their duty but came under pressure not to print a list of names for fear of embarrassing those who had not joined up for active service. "We are informed it might be invidious to do so as there are some who would gladly have volunteered if domestic and business affairs did not prevent it."[16] Nevertheless they were able to record that 2 officers and 30 NCOs and men had volunteered out of a (revised) complement of 52 .

The patriotism of these Territorials was as might be expected heartily applauded by local dignitaries and held up as an example to others when the recruiting meetings got underway. In Cellardyke Sir Ralph Anstruther and his son Henry were cheered when they arrived by motor car to join the platform, from which Provost Black praised the Territorials but also had to draw attention to the loutish behaviour of local youths saying "he was sorry to hear that a few of their young men had been heard sneering and jeering at the noble stand made by their Territorials".[17]

(Such behaviour was not apparently unheard of. A similar recruiting event in West Calder, West Lothian was disrupted when a large number of drunks mixed with the crowd and interrupted the speakers.)

Despite the foreboding of what the war may cost there was little obvious reluctance in sending Anstruther's sons to war and over the next year there were constant exhortations for volunteers to join up. Although many opted for the local regiment the Royal Highlanders (Black Watch), adverts appeared in the local press for the Fife and Forfar Yeomanry, Royal Field Artillery and the Highland Cyclists Battalion, in whose ranks Anstruther and Cellardyke men would serve and fall. Opportunities arose or were pressed on men who might have initially been turned away. The advert for the 17th Battalion The Royal Scots in the *East of Fife Record* proclaimed "You cannot now advance the excuse that you are below the standard height, for this battalion has been specially formed to meet your

---

[15] Dennis p29
[16] CBO 20 August 1914
[17] CBO 20 Aug 1914

case - join the famous Bantams."[18]

If we look forward however to the the first anniversary of the war, by that time there were signs that the town felt it had done its bit. A Great Final Rally to the Colours was announced with 33 musicians of the New Army recruiting band. Captain Steven the recruiting officer clearly believed that there were volunteers who had not heard or heeded the call. The *East of Fife Record* did not disagree although it was beginning to wonder how useful such appeals were likely to be. "No one will deny that in our neighbourhood there still remains a few for whom the tocsin has sounded in vain. Taking Fife as the recruiting area there was at the time of the last census close on 30,000 men of fighting age. Since the war broke out 50% have enlisted and what the recruiting agents would like to know is where have the remaining half of the men gone to?"[19]

Yet the failure of the rally- which recruited only 4 volunteers - did not cause the paper to condemn local men as shirkers but instead to change its tone and conclude that the recruiters were wasting their time. "This continual beating up of a district that has already given of its best is beginning to have an irritating effect... why cannot these recruiters get busy in an area where plenty of men are still available."[20]

Certainly the feeling was that Anstruther and Cellardyke had contributed more than their fair share. However it was never entirely clear exactly how many had enlisted. Early in the war the local paper had wanted to print a Roll of Honour of those who had signed up, taking as its lead the village of Kippen, Stirlingshire which had by October 1914 honoured their local volunteers with a vellum record. But there was apparently no public record of the local recruits and the paper depended upon relatives sending in names of those who had joined up or were already serving. The first such list appeared in October 22 1914 and was reprinted and added to over the next few weeks but did not reappear after the turn of the year.

Whilst mobilisation of forces for the trenches was going on, men were also leaving to serve at sea - in the last week of September 1914, Cellardyke alone sent 20 men to Portsmouth. Amid even more emotional scenes than had sent the Territorials on their way, they departed from Anstruther railway station. The station platforms were overwhelmed by

---

[18] EoFR 22 April 1915

[19] EoFR 19 August 1915

[20] EoFR 2 September 1915

17

relatives and friends to the extent that many had to be content with shouting their goodbyes from the road. The departure meant that already 70 men had joined up from Cellardyke out of a population of around 3000, and more continued to leave - the following week another 6 and a fortnight later a further 15. Off they went carrying their familiar Cellardyke names. A Martin Gardner was one of the first to go - a name which could trace its presence in the fishing records back to the 16th century. He was joined in October 1914 by two other Gardners, both called Robert. Off too went Watsons and Betts, Andersons and Tarvits.

Although it may seem entirely to be expected that a community dominated by fishing should have close links with the navy, in fact the number of Reservists amongst the fishermen was felt not just to be to be surprisingly low but it was believed that no East Neuk fishermen were members of the RNR at all. So what about the 40 or so local fishermen who had to report to Methil immediately on the outbreak of war? In fact these were not Cellardyke men but half-dealsmen from the West Highlands and Islands who were part of the naval reserve. With the exception of men from that area there was otherwise a wide Scottish disinterest in the Royal Naval Reserve which had lost support throughout the fishing fleet after the initial idea of training men at shore stations close to their homes was dropped in favour of training taking place on board naval vessels at sea.

Like the Territorials the problem was of the time commitment to training which in the naval reservists' case was even more onerous. Reservists were required to devote 14 weeks en bloc to their first period of training. Furthermore this absence often clashed with the herring drave making patriotic service financially particularly unattractive to East Neuk men.

After the outbreak of war fishing was badly affected and with boats confined to harbour, the young men had time (and perhaps also the financial stimulus) to sign up for the Reserve.

Certainly by the end of 1914 when no fishing had been allowed for 3 months the attraction of £2 per week wages for a deckhand serving with the drifter patrol was prominent in the recruitment publicity, and was enough at the turn of the year to tempt another 10 local men to war. Skippers earned 9/- per day; second hands and enginemen 6/-; deckhands 3/6d and trimmers 3/- plus they were provided with full kit and a small allowance for upkeep.[21]

---

[21] EoFR 21 August 1914

Just the kit could be enough for some. A young George Watson went off to Methil to enlist, attracted by the thought that the smart new uniform would impress the girls back in Cellardyke. (His parents' fury at the starry-eyed impetuousness of their too young son would have been heightened by the sight of the tattoos which he acquired at the same time - with the tattooist recommending that he bite into the rim of his cap to stifle the pain.)[22]

But clearly it was not just for the money or the glamour that over two thirds of Scotland's fishermen served in the war. A survey taken in 1917 showed that of the total of 33,000 men whose usual occupation was fishing, 10,292 were on minesweeping or patrol duties; 6,253 were in the navy and 1,645 in the army.[23]

Petty Officer Fred Blunsdon, killed when submarine D5 hit a mine.

---

[22] Pers.comm.

[23] Jones p.85

However the first local naval casualties came not from the enthusiastic throng volunteering their services but from those who had joined up with the Regular forces many years before.

On 3 October 1914 the British submarine D5, under the command of Captain Herbert, left the port of Yarmouth on patrol. It had seen action in the early days of the war having fired 2 torpedoes at the German cruiser Rostock on 22 August both however passing beneath the target. Off Lowestoft D5 hit a mine.

Caught in the explosion was Petty Officer Frederick Blunsdon aged 31. A Regular in the Navy, he lived with his wife Rose in Southsea, Portsmouth and had already survived an explosion in another submarine which had blown him out through the conning tower and into the sea, injuring him severely. This time the blast was fatal. He became the first Anstruther man to be reported killed in the First World War (and the first of many to die from mine explosions). The local paper in reporting his death was careful to note that his elderly parents who lived in Tolbooth Wynd in Anstruther Easter had not yet been informed by the authorities more than a month after the event. It accorded PO Blunsdon what turned out to be a relatively rare honour of printing his photograph and noting with a degree of formality that he was well known and highly esteemed in Anstruther (although somewhat spoiling the recognition by spelling his name different ways in the reports and captions).

A month later another local Regular seaman was in trouble. Stoker George Robertson, with 7 years service in the Royal Navy, found himself on the other side of the world trying to force one last effort from the crippled engines of his ship, *HMS Monmouth*.

At Coronel, 50 miles off the coast of Chile, the *Monmouth* was silhouetted on the skyline at sunset, providing an unmissable target for the powerful German cruiser *Gneisenau*. She was shelled at a distance of 12,000 yards and was on fire within minutes. The British ship, built twelve years previously, had found its fourteen 6 inch guns "manned almost exclusively by reservists" could not be worked in the heavy seas and were in any case no match for the German squadron which also included the cruiser *Scharnhorst*. In what was to be seen as a heroic effort to draw the fire away from *HMS Good Hope* (which, however, was sunk) and *HMS Glasgow*, the *Monmouth* sent a last signal saying "Am making water badly forward. Engines disabled and in a sinking condition but am making towards the enemy to try and torpedo her." However she had become a " wallowing funeral pyre"[24] and sailors on *HMS Glasgow* making their escape were sickened at the sight and sound of an unanswered 75 flashes from the German attackers and then silence.

Stoker George Robertson, lost on HMS Monmouth

The coup de grace was executed by the the German ship *Nurnberg*, which came up close to the defenceless *Monmouth*, which was listing so badly that even if any guns could be operated, they could not be brought to bear on the enemy. However her engines were still running (so Stoker Robertson was still perhaps hard at work) and her flag was still flying. The *Nurnberg* fired at a distance of no more than 1,000 yards and then stopped to see if *Monmouth* would run down her colours and so surrender. She did not and indeed seemed to turn towards the German ship in an effort either to ram her or bring her starboard guns to bear. A final salvo from the *Nurnberg* was fired, ripping open *Monmouth's* side and she slowly capsized. All hands were lost on 1 November 1914, including 25 year old Stoker Robertson, in what was Britain's first defeat at sea for a hundred years.[25] Back home at Volum Cottage in the week

---

[24] Hough p95
[25] Keegan p233

before Christmas his father, William Robertson sent a letter of acknowledgement to his fellow councillors of Anstruther Wester Town Council which, not for the last time, had sent a message of condolence to one of its own. Not all such deaths were the result of enemy action. As Cellardyke knew only too well the sea could claim men all by itself.

In February 1915 the *Clan Macnaughton* disappeared in the north Atlantic taking with her a crew of nearly 300 including William Reekie a 22 year old Naval Reservist from Cellardyke.[26] This was a disaster and many suspected that the ship had foundered not just because of the bitter sea conditions. The *Clan MacNaughton* was a new ship - it had been built in Glasgow in 1911. However it was a merchant vessel and had to be converted for naval duties with guns and armour plating. Had the weight of these alterations destabilised the ship and caused it to founder? An inquiry was ordered and a statement was made to the House of Commons a month after the ship was presumed to have gone down. The Admiralty was said to be satisfied that the vessel was in good condition and seaworthy and that she possessed ample stability, stressing that the

William Reekie's ship disappeared with all hands in the Atlantic

---

[26] William Reekie is reported as part of a contingent heading off for the naval reserve from Cellardyke - CBO 11.10.1914

armaments placed on the ship were light in comparison to her size.[27]

The sea rather than enemy attack was also to blame when a month later another 22 year old from Cellardyke was being mourned after five members of the crew of the patrol boat *Coreopsis,* stationed at Larne, were swept into the water off the Irish coast at Antrim. Accounts of what happened differ, as they so often do in war. Newspapers reported the heroic efforts made by the boat's engineer to save the men and four were rescued but despite diving repeatedly into the sea he was unable to save deckhand John Bett who drowned. After four hours of searching his body was recovered and he was brought home to be buried at Kilrenny churchyard. His family were left to wonder why he had been endangered in the first place having been told that he had been put into a small boat to recover an anchor and, in the middle of a gale, the boat had capsized.

The *Coreopsis* was a fishing boat, a drifter, which had been requisitioned by the Admiralty for patrol work. Many Cellardyke and Anstruther boats were to be similarly taken into service. By 1917 over 1,100 Scottish fishing boats had been taken into Admiralty service of which 53, all steam drifters or liners, came from Anstruther district (which covered Anstruther, Cellardyke, Pittenweem and St Monans.)[28]

The war had brought difficult conditions for the East Neuk fishing industry. *The Scotsman* newspaper reported that even as early as 4 August 1914 'the summer fishing has been brought to a complete standstill' five or six weeks earlier than usual. In part this was because of the departure of the half-dealsmen. There seems also to have been a problem with securing insurance. By the turn of the year fishing was being allowed only within a restricted area. Under the Defence of the Realm Act boats were not allowed to fish west of an imaginary line drawn from Crail to the Isle of May and through to Dunbar. (Not in this case for fear of enemy action but as much for getting in the way of military activity in the Forth estuary which teemed with craft coming from Rosyth.) An exception was made for those boats under 35ft in length which were allowed to line fish between Kirkcaldy and Crail but only if they stayed within half a mile of of the low water mark.

Local skippers were regularly in court for flouting the rules. In early March 1915 Martin Gardner skipper of the steam drifter *Vanguard III*, 18 Fowler Street, Cellardyke was fined £3 with the option of 15 days

[27] CBO 4.3.1915
[28] Jones p84

imprisonment; John Muir (Keay) 29 Shore Street Cellardyke , skipper of *Camperdown*; Thomas Bett, 3 Fowler Street , skipper of the *Scot* and Henry Bett of the same address in charge of the *Breadwinner* were fined £1 each or 5 days as was Robert Anderson of Burnside Terrace, skipper of the *Sunbeam*. In all 40 cases came to court that day and the warning was issued that if the contraventions continued then fishing would have to be stopped.

Vanguard III whose Skipper Martin Gardner was fined for breaching fishing restrictions in March 1915, before his boat was requisitioned by the Navy

But before the month was out more Cellardyke fishermen were in court. Alexander Lothian (*Snowflight*); Thomas Bett (*Cornucopia*) Leslie Jack (*Suffolk County*); William Smith (*Olive Leaf*) were all fined £3 or 15 days. However John Wilson, the skipper of the *Ruby*, who lived at 28 Shore Street was admonished when the Fiscal reported that he had three sons on active service, two in the army and one in the navy. (The Sheriff's leniency was little compensation for the later loss of both of the sons who were soldiers. John died with the Black Watch. George, previously a plumber with Gray and Pringle had emigrated to Canada, and became a sergeant, falling with the Alberta Regiment 31st Battalion Canadian Infantry.) In the first year of the war the five Fishery Board cruisers which had been put at the disposal of the Admiralty made 10,000 boardings of boats in the Forth.[29] Throughout 1915 and into 1916 the fisherman were regularly brought before the court. The local press reported yet another last warning to the skippers and feared that those who were being tempted beyond the line were jeopardising the prospects of the "great majority loyally observing the restrictions."[30]

In September 1915 a mass meeting of fishermen was held at Buckhaven. They were furious at the Admiralty action which meant that so many of their number were being criminalised at Cupar Sheriff Court. They disagreed that there was any threat arising from their fishing activities. But these protestations did not stop skippers being hauled before the courts. Some tried to blame the weather. James Bowman claimed that the reason why he was caught fishing outside the half-mile limit was that a gale was blowing off the land and his engine refused to work. This was contradicted by the torpedo boat commander who said the sea was calm and there was nothing wrong with the motor. The verdict? Guilty - pay £5 or spend 30 days in prison. Rarely did anyone escape punishment although James Jack of 25 John Street, fishing from his boat *Expert* got off with an admonishment in April 1916 when the court accepted that he was fishing for personal consumption.

The aggrieved fishermen had presented their case not just as individual grievance but as one of social concern. More fish would reduce prices they argued and thus relieve the burden on poorer people. And if the fishing was closed as was threatened there was no alternative employment for the older men on the boats - provision would have to be made for them. (Presumably they had not taken kindly to the suggestion carried in the Dundee *Courier* that Fife fishermen who could not fish due to the war should spend their time making toy fishing boats.[31]) The restrictions were indeed having an effect on fish catches. In July 1915 the *East of Fife Record* reported that the catch of herring in the previous month for the whole of Scotland had declined by 96%. Official figures show that the East Coast summer herring fishing was drastically down on comparable period prior to the war. The 1913 catch was 2,300,00 cwt; in 1915 only 60,000 cwt was landed by Scottish boats and prices doubled.[32] Catches of all other kinds of fish (e.g. whiting) fell by 41% but the value was actually higher by 10%.[33]

---

[29] Jones p42

[30] EoFR 22.7.1915

[31] CBO 8.10.1914

[32] Jones

[33] EoFR 29.7.1915

However the cost was even higher in boats lost and in human lives. In June 1915 alone it was reported that 51 British trawlers were destroyed by German submarines - all in the North Sea.[34] The East Neuk fishing boats were about to confront such perils but on patrol or minesweeping duties as, like the *Coreopsis,* they were requisitioned by the Admiralty. The *Scot* and the *Vanguard III* were away, two months after they had landed their skippers in court and by the end of May 1915 over 40 local drifters had been taken for the patrol service. Many of the boats would come back to fishing at the end of the war, although some like The *Morning Star* and *Evening Star* had to have their keels and planking replaced because of the ravages of service in the Mediterranean. A couple however would be lost including the *Craignoon*, a 77 ton drifter built in 1904 which was sunk by gunfire in May 1917 in the Adriatic.

---

[34] EoFR 19.8.1915

Chapter 3

'Anstruther Heavily Hit'

If a Navy regular was the first local man to die, the first Anstruther man reported to fall in the trenches was also a Regular. Thomas Swan (26) served with the Black Watch 2nd battalion which had, for years, been based at Fort William in Calcutta. Life was dominated by training, sports and grand ceremonials and the occasional soldiering. The 2nd battalion had, for instance, furnished the Guard of Honour arranged on the steps of the throne when King George V was crowned King-Emperor in New Delhi in December 1911. When it came to sports Swan was a capable athlete, winning the hurdles in the battalion games in January 1913 and repeating the victory in the regimental games in December 1913 with a precisely recorded winning time of 18 and two-fifth seconds. Military necessity got in the way of sport when the Black Watch had to contribute to a show of strength to suppress sedition in Dacca. Clearly the kilted troops were already proud of their to-be-feared reputation amongst the local people as 'langte gore' - unclothed soldiers. By February 1914 it was back to sport and the pinnacle of the sub-continents challenge, the Highland Brigade gathering. Thousands of soldiers from the Black Watch, Camerons, Seaforths, Argyll and Sutherland Highlanders, and Gordon Highlanders gathered in Agra. Thomas Swan lined up for the 120 yard hurdles in the natural amphitheatre "overshadowed by the domes and minarets of the famous Taj Mahal at one end and the splendid view of the Agra Fort with the glistening domes of the Pearl Mosque at the other end."[35] He came a creditable third in the event, with the Black Watch coming second to the Seaforths in the overall standings at the end of three days competition.

When war came Swan embarked at Karachi on 21st September 1914 with the rest of the Indian Contingent. It was said that the men on the *SS Elephanta* were so keen to see action in France that they volunteered as stokers. Whether that is true or not, they reached Marseilles in a month.

It was not long before the Black Watch Regulars distinguished themselves in action in the Battle of Festubert. On the morning of 23rd November the Germans made a heavy attack along almost the whole front of the Indian Corps. The strength of the assault breached the British defences but instead of pulling back, 50 men of the 2nd battalion Black Watch

---

[35] Black Watch Chronicle 1914 p211

organised a counterattack to assist the 58th Rifles in retaking the trenches from which they had just been forced. Battling across snow-covered ground the British could be easily picked out and casualties were severe. Swan and two other NCOs were decorated for their part in the action.[36]

Lance Corporal Thomas Swan DCM.

However he was never to be presented with his Distinguished Conduct Medal. At the beginning of December 1914 he was back in the trenches opposite Festubert. Here the opposing front lines came close to touching - a 300 yards stretch ran parallel to and only 12 yards apart from the German trenches - and one particularly exposed point, The Glory Hole, was only 12 feet from the German lines and had to be held against constant bombing attacks. As the Black Watch historian drily noted "... the fighting resolved itself in a great measure to fighting with grenades. In this the Germans were superior both in equipment and training".[37] Lance Corporal Swan (just promoted for the first time in his nine years service) was killed on 5 December 1914.

---

[36] Merewether and Smith p131

[37] Wauchope Vol. 1 p170

(His mother Elizabeth finally received his DCM almost exactly a year later at her home in Chalmers House.)

Another man who travelled thousands of miles to fight and die on the Western Front was 21 year old Corporal James Murray of the Canadian Highlanders, Central Ontario Regiment. His parents Robert and Lucy lived at 4 Shore Street, Cellardyke and had been waiting anxiously to hear from their son after a fellow soldier had written to tell them he was in hospital in Rouen. In fact he had been killed on April 22 and is commemorated on the Menin Gate memorial, Ypres. Robert Murray was proud of being a Canadian - his grieving parents erected a headstone with a maple leaf to his memory in Kilrenny churchyard.

Emigration from the East Neuk to Canada had been actively promoted pre war. Adverts ran regularly in the local press. 'Go ahead Canada wants go-ahead young men - and guarantees work on the land and for domestic servants at good wages.' For farmers Ontario boasted '25 million acres of virgin soil at 2/- per acre' (although by 1914 the attractions seemed to have waned with reports that the number emigrating were infinitesimal compared with what it was recently and emigrants were complaining that work had never been so scarce.) Many emigrant Scots joined up and Corporal Murray was the first of seven local men to die in Canadian uniform.

Others who travelled far to fight never saw the Western Front. Turkey had entered the war against the Allies in October 1914, but it had not been expected that British troops would be committed to another front. However deadlock in Flanders meant that there was little prospect of an early end to war. The thoughts of Churchill and Kitchener turned towards the Dardanelles where it was hoped the naval strength of Britain could be used to make military gains and also support the Russian's efforts to seize Constantinople. The result was disaster. The main assault took place in April 1915 and after being massacred on the beaches of Gallipoli the Allied forces were pinned down for months. Two Anstruther men died in that time. William Watson was a stoker who found himself on dry land with a rifle in his hand with the Hood Battalion of the Royal Navy Division. At 11.20 am on the 4 June 1915 he would have been yelling and waving his bayonet above the parapet of his trench, at the conclusion of an Allied bombardment. This was not out of any high spirits but cheering to order as part of a ruse to persuade the Turkish forces that an infantry attack had started and so to tempt them out of their shelter and into the frontline where they would again be shelled by the artillery. At noon the Royal Naval Division stormed out of their trenches and despite capturing the enemy frontline were cut down - within a short time Watson was one of 1,300 RND casualties. One observer described " tumbled heaps of khaki everywhere. Scores and scores of them looking like dead leaves in autumn."[38]

William Moncrieff also lost his life. The 35 year old Royal Scots private, whose parents home was in Shore Street Cellardyke, left behind his wife Anne, in Gordon Street in Leith. He had already confronted death on his way to war when he "escaped scathless"[39] from the Gretna rail disaster, Britain's worst ever, which saw 210 of his comrades killed or burnt to death. Ironically this carnage meant that the Royal Scots arrived too late to take part in the 4 June attack but the delay did not save Moncrieff who died before the month was out.

In an attempt to achieve a breakthrough a further amphibious assault was ordered. Troops were gathered on the Greek island of Lemnos and on 7 August 1915 were launched into Suvla Bay on the Gallipoli peninsula. They were swelling forces which had already been cooped up for months, including the Australian Light Horse which for eleven weeks had been digging trenches or ferrying supplies and now wanted to get into battle.

The task the Australians were given was simple and suicidal - to charge the Turk trenches "across a ridge so narrow only 150 men could advance at a time, in broad daylight, with the sun in their eyes at point blank range..."[40] Within 15 minutes 3 waves of attack had been made by the Australians - who suffered 50% casualties out of the 1,250 officers and men who took part. Amongst them was Lance Corporal William Tosh (28) who had left Fife some 10 years previously to take up sheep farming. He came from relatively well-to-do stock. His late father had farmed at Thirdpart between Anstruther and Crail. Tosh, and his widowed mother lived at 'Mansefield' Anstruther.

His death was reported not just in the local press but in the columns of *The Scotsman*, which recorded that he had been educated at Clifton Bank School, St Andrews, and after a business training in a solicitor's office in Anstruther he had learnt sheep farming near Kelso in preparation for going to Australia.

---

[38] Rhodes James pp211 - 213

[39] EoFR 20 April 1916. His brother Alex was killed a year later fighting in a Canadian contingent but his name does not appear on the Anstruther or Cellardyke memorial.

[40] Rhodes James p211

His death achieved nothing; there was to be no end to the stalemate. For a few months more the Allies hung on, in conditions which can scarcely be imagined.

Lance Corporal William Tosh, killed in Gallipoli

In the summer heat men died from dysentery, and the stench from overflowing latrines, as well as from unburied corpses assailed the trenches which were infested with flies, lice and maggots; in the late autumn of 1915 a storm flooded the trenches drowning men and animals; and in winter sentries froze at their posts. And all the time the attrition continued. A local soldier gave his account of landing in the Dardanelles.

"About a mile from the shore we were met by fire of all kinds, shrapnel machine gun fire and rifle. Our young Lieutenant was shot through the head. I am no navvy but when I touched dry ground I seemed to have been a navvy all of my life the way I took a pick and shovel and dug myself in... we had a hot time especially the first fortnight when I went about without a shave, a wash or without taking off my clothes. Out of our 40, our casualties averaged 3 a day. It seemed as if we all had to go...one would be working alongside a chap when suddenly he would fall. Shouts were raised for the stretcher bearers then continue to work until the next fell."[41]

---

[41] EoFR 21 October 1915

By the end of the year Gallipoli was being evacuated by the Allies, having cost a quarter of a million men killed, wounded and missing.[42]

By contrast the first of the Anstruther Territorials to die in uniform never left Fife. Robert Watson is reported as having contracted a chill on manoeuvres. The 21 year old was brought home to 17 James Street where he succumbed to what was officially registered as pulmonary phthisis. A squad of Territorials from the reserve 2/7 Black Watch, under Sergeant Watt, was sent from the camp at Kinghorn to represent the regiment at his funeral, April 1915. "Although not of a robust constitution he threw himself eagerly into the work of training" the local paper sympathetically noted.[43]

His own 1/7th Btn colleagues could not be present as, shortly beforehand they had been despatched from Fife to camp in England. Before departing they had the opportunity to put their affairs in order. One of those to do so was Lance Corporal Willie Watson who worked in the family oilskin clothing factory in George Street, Cellardyke. The firm, Robt. Watson & Co. Ltd., had been founded by his grandfather in 1859. Willie lived with his parents at 'Craigholm', a solid detached house in Ladywalk, Anstruther Easter which faced onto what is now the Bankie Park. He was a well known face in the community. A keen sportsman he played golf, bowls and tennis, but his real passion was as a pigeon fancier. With his older brother Robert he kept a loft and he would spend hours there trying to breed the perfect bird. When his brother and his family were away on holiday in Bridge of Earn in July 1914, Willie had filled four pages of a letter to him describing the condition of the birds and his hopes for the young ones as they developed - this on top of having updated Robert by telephone earlier in the week.

On 7 April 1915 Willie had gone into Kirkcaldy and signed a will drawn up by his solicitors Mackintosh and Watson in which he left his whole estate to his father. The will was witnessed by his friend George Cunningham who was also in the Black Watch Territorials. Cunningham's father was a ships chandler and their family home was 'Glenogle' on the Crail Road which could be seen directly across the park from Willie's house.

A few days later the two young men were in camp in Bedford. There the men were involved in square bashing. Willie wrote to his sister-in-law

---

[42] Keegan p268
[43] EoFR 22 April 1915

32

Aggie Watson, "We have a hard time of it here having no less than 8 parades per day, starting at 6 o'clock in the morning and finishing at 6 o'clock at night."

Bedford was packed with troops ready to go war and there was rivalry between them. New recruits for the Gordons were found to be "badly wanting, not being inoculated and not having their musketry put in so we don't now how long they will keep us back." By contrast he felt that his own regiment drew grudging admiration from the others: "they all give in that we are the biggest and heaviest battalion that has come to Bedford, not bad for the despised 7th"[44]

(It was not just the 7th Black Watch which was "despised" but Territorials in general. Kitchener had no time for the Territorials which were recruited and serviced by County Associations. The Territorials were aggrieved that Kitchener's New Army was clearly being favoured above them. On August 8 immediately on becoming Secretary of State for War he had issued a call to arms, appealing for 100,000 volunteers to come forward and join his New Army. By the end of the war 404 New Army battalions had seen active service compared to 318 Territorial battalions. The Territorials were deprived of trainers, equipment and above all official favour and publicity).[45]

Being part of such a throng was a laugh, especially on occasions like bathing parade when the men were drawn up at the swimming baths down at the river. "It was great fun. 200 men in at one time. You had hardly room to move and was almost drowned with the jabble."

But they were there to go to war and rumours were rife and nerves were taut. We get a good insight into what it was like from another letter from Willie to his brother: "I was just going to bed at 11 o'clock when the alarm was sounded. I slipped on my kilt and rushed out to see what was up. There was Maxwell and Macintosh (Capt. Charles Maxwell the Anstruther town clerk and Lieut. Hugh MacIntosh) knocking the men up ... we were all paraded and were told that a scare had got about and were to pack up in marching order ready to move at a moments notice."[46] The scare was that the battalion might be needed in France (or "the danger sphere" as Willie put it.) The instruction was given that a man should stay awake in each hut to listen out for the alarm, which is why

[44] Letter to Aggie Watson 25.4.1915

[45] Dennis p31

[46] Letter to Robert Watson 22 April 1915

Willie found himself writing to his brother at 12.45am. However he was aware that even if nothing came of this alert, going to the front was imminent. The Black Watch knew that the Gordon Highlanders who were in the same brigade as them were due to go the following Monday. Furthermore their kit had been taken away leaving them only with their fighting kit - 2 shirts, 2 pairs of socks, shaving set, 2 towels, soap and a woollen helmet. "Not much you will think" said Willie "but quite enough to carry on one's back along with 150 pounds ball cartridge, overcoat and equipment." Training was now focussed on trying to get them ready for the front-line. The men were taken to an obstacle course and practised "jumping trenches, scaling 12 or 15 feet barricades, crawling through barbed wire entanglements, running through stakes and sundry other feats."

In the middle of the night the implications of what was to come clearly hung in the air. Furthermore Willie had only that day learned of the death of Robert Watson (" wee Bob" as he called him). He had spent the hours writing to his father and his other brother Geordie and as he signed off his letter to his brother Robert he said "If I'm lucky enough to get home again the three of us must have a good holiday. I'm lucky having brothers like you."

On 2 May Willie had time to dash off a postcard to Robert letting him know that they were about to travel down to Folkestone to be shipped at once to Boulogne - marvelling at the prospect that " this time tomorrow we will be on foreign soil."

The next Sunday morning, 9 May he wrote of how they had finally got underway at 4 o'clock in the afternoon and by midnight were in France. "We slept a night in bivouacks (sic) and then came up to a place inland here in a cattle truck. We came out of the truck at some town or other and made a night march to a farm where we were quartered for a day or two and then made another night march to a farm which is a few miles from the trenches."[47]

Willie had a good eye for detail and noted "there are few signs of war here except the cannonading and the soldiers all about here, but one significant thing is you very seldom see any Frenchman between the age of 19 and 40 and the farm work seems entirely done by women, old men and boys." The presence of foreign troops caught his eye. "We enjoyed the sight this morning of a regiment of Indian Lancers passing the farm... with their dark

---

[47] Letter to Robert Watson 9 May 1915

warlike faces and huge turbans bestriding their superb horses."

He betrayed the innocence of not yet having any combat experience and reflected Imperial hubris by saying "I don't wonder at the enemy turning tail at the sight of them." He repeated the theme by sending a picture postcard to his young nephew Alick, of Senegalese tirailleurs. These were colonial troops in the French army. They were highly distinctive in their voluminous, billowing trousers. However the black and white photo taken in 1914 does not do justice to their colourful tunics piped (at that time) with yellow lace at the cuffs and collars. As Willie pointed out to the young boy "they have got awful wide breeks but they can fairly go for the Germans with their big knives."[48]

The excitement of being in France, the fine weather and the theatrical presence of the foreign troops kept Willie's spirits high and he signed off his first letter saying "I'm feeling champion." The officer's scrawl at the bottom of the letter is that of Capt. Maxwell who clearly saw nothing to warrant his censor's pencil.

A week later and he was closer to the action but had not yet reached the frontline trenches. He seemed unsure of their role. "We seem to be some sort of Reserve or other and our job seems to be to keep immediately behind the firing line and anywhere in the line reinforcements are likely to be wanted we seem to be marched to. We have made 4 good marches since we came out here."

After only a fortnight in France his letter conveys homesickness - he talks to his brother about their pigeons; asks how the tennis and bowling is going on and says he "often sits and pictures the green with all the local worthies enjoying themselves to their hearts content." He looks forward to making up for lost time and returns to the fond hope of going away on holiday with his brothers "if I'm lucky and get home again." It is difficult to know whether he thought it really would take luck to survive or that it would tempt fate to expect to come through unharmed.

On 20 May he wrote to his brother again complaining that "we have had some rotten night marches lately and as it has been practically raining for the last 3 days steady, it's no joke plodding through the wet and darkness." Clearly this was a miserable experience. "You will have no idea what like a night march is. You stumble along in the darkness, stumbling in all the inequalities of the ground and bumping into the man

---

48 Postcard to Alick Watson 15 May 1915

in front. You march until you are half dazed with weariness and sleep, then in the small hours of the morning you stumble into some farm byre among straw, tumble down, get your coat out of your pack, spread it over you the best way you can in the darkness and sleep like the dead until 7.30." The previous night had been made even more miserable because at midnight they had been forced to sit down in the middle of the road for an hour in the rain.

His thoughts were now clearly of home: " you don't know how I would enjoy a trot round the lofts and 21 ends on the green, a set or two of tennis, 15 holes on Earlsferry and all the list of luxuries I used to enjoy."

He wanted to let his brother know that he was about to go into action and the letter is laden with hints saying that he just had time to write before proceeding to "business" (underlined) and that he might not get another letter written for some time but would get one home as soon as possible. Normally he just ended his letter simply by signing his name. This time he closed unusually by wishing Robert "good luck". But of course it was Willie who needed luck.

The next night Willie Watson and the rest of the 7th Battalion Black Watch reached the frontline for the first time. They were to have their baptism of fire in what was officially regarded as the Battle of Festubert.

The history of the Black Watch records:

"During the night of May 21st the 7th Btn relieved the 6th in the Festubert sector. Here the trenches ran through an uncleared battlefield and the whole area was littered with arms, tools and the unburied bodies of both British and German soldiers. Even a few wounded men were still lying in the open, and the task of the battalion in clearing the battlefield and holding the line was a heavy one."[49]

The headline in the *East of Fife Record* reflected this: 'Casualties Suffered in First Spell of Trenches - Anstruther Heavily Hit' . The accompanying text however opened more like an account of a hard fought rugby match, speaking of the Territorials having 'put in an exciting time before leaving for a rest spell, losing 5 men killed and 19 wounded.'[50]

Lance Corporal Willie Watson was in charge of No.2 Section 14 Platoon

---

[49] Wauchope p251
[50] EoFR 3 June 1915

D Company which was out during the night of 23 May trying to establish a new trench 'troubled only by intermittent shrapnel and star shells'. However towards morning their position came under direct attack and the digging party was ordered to withdraw to their original position.

Willie did not make it. He and another Anstruther Lance Corporal Alex Robb were hit before they could reach the trenches. Willie Watson was killed, the first Anstruther Territorial to die in action. He had been in France just 21 days and in the front line for just over 48 hours.

Lance Corporal Willie Watson,
the first local Territorial to be killed.

Their parents were written to by their Commanding Officer, Captain Maxwell. He tried to bring comfort to Watson's father whom he clearly knew well:

"My Dear Friend, You will try to take it bravely if you have not had the news from another source. Willie was killed in action early this morning (24 May). He died instantaneously and we buried him where he fell. My thoughts are with you and my whole heart goes out to you."

Although it was almost a convention to reassure parents that their son had suffered no pain it is likely to be the case for Willie Watson for, by contrast, Maxwell unusually let the parents of Robb know the distressing circumstances of their son's death. He wrote:

"I cannot sufficiently express my sorrow on learning that Alex has died of the wounds he received on Monday morning. After a fusillade of shrapnel I heard sounds of distress from in front of the trench and on getting the man in we found he was your son - very severely wounded in the head and arm...your son was a first class soldier and when your grief has lessened you will have a proud memory of a dutiful son who laid down his life to help his country in its hour of need·"[51]

(Alex Robb was only 19. A railwayman, he lived with his parents at School Wynd. By the end of the war Alex and Margaret Robb could be justifiably proud of the contribution their sons had made as another, John, a sapper was to receive the Military Medal for removing a field gun from a dangerous position "whilst the enemy rained fire on him.")[52]

For the parents the bureaucracy of death then visited them. On 9 June an official notification of Willie being killed in action was issued by Colonel Elliot in the Perth Territorial Force Record Office; on 2nd July he forwarded exact details of where Willie was buried; and on 15 July the official certificate of death was despatched from London.

After Willie had written his last letter to his brother on the 20 May he had written into his pay book a will bequeathing all his property and effects to his father (notwithstanding the will which he had taken the time to have drawn up before he left camp at Kinghorn.) On 18th September Alex Watson was sent five pounds one shilling and sixpence in settlement.

The deaths of the Territorials seems to mark a turning point in the way that Anstruther experienced the war. The community had not been insulated from the conflict - local men had previously died and others from the area had already returned home injured. They knew the scale of war. However the Regulars were not only professional soldiers but they had also been away from the community for years on end, as had those fighting for Canadian and Australian forces. The Territorials by contrast would have been familiar faces - ordinary men in ordinary jobs,

---

[51] EoFR 3 June 1915

[52] EFO 28 March 1918.

now placed in extraordinary danger. They had gone willingly out of a sense of patriotic duty .

At Willie Watson's memorial service at the Chalmers church it was recalled that as he left Kinghorn to go to war he said, " Do you not think it is the duty of every young man to take his share in this great cause?"

The death of the Territorials in their first foray to the Front provided bitter confirmation that Anstruther and Cellardyke were doing their bit and were sharing in the sacrifice. However in looking for someone to embody honour and preparedness for self sacrifice, the local paper did not focus on Watson or Robb but rather the man who broke the news of their death.

Captain Maxwell's active service record is brief and is not distinguished by any awards for valour. That is not to say that he was not a committed leader of his men. On the night the two Anstruther men died, another local Territorial, Lance Corporal Anderson, who was one of those wounded said of Maxwell, " Last night he went out of our trenches and brought in a chap who belonged to St Andrews who was lying severely wounded. The bullets were flying about Captain Maxwell all the time but he came back without a scratch."

Such a testimony provided the base for a fulsome and somewhat over done pean of praise from the Reverend Urquhart who, in the presence of Maxwell's wife at the opening of the annual Sunday School picnic, acclaimed her husband for having "done things even at his early stage of military experience according to his own men which were worthy of the Victoria Cross. The men who had returned home said they were willing to do anything even die for Captain Maxwell."[53]

The following month the paper reported that Captain Maxwell had a narrow escape with his life, "A German bullet grazed his cheek too closely to be pleasant"[54], an experience which however unwelcome must have been commonplace to soldiers of whatever rank.

Maxwell's own view of the war seems to have been ambivalent - certainly he regarded it as a curse but nevertheless he felt it had a profound positive effect on those who experienced it. "War is a great purifier and when our youth return home the weed will be non existent and in his place

---

[53] EoFR 15 July 1915

[54] EoFR 19 August 1915

you will find a disciplined self reliant man."[55]

This distinction between the men who had endured the character building experience of military service and those who whinged at home over their circumstances was not for him just a personal opinion or typical of his own class, but one he believed shared by all ranks. He expressed his views vehemently: "the only thing that makes our fellows sick at heart and discouraged is the news that working people are striking for some paltry advance in wages. When they heard about the Welsh miners the common wish of the battalion was that they should be sent home to quell the strike".[56] (The Welsh miners had gone on strike in July 1915 to enforce the closed shop.)[57]

It may be that the farm estate and fishing trades workers of east Fife felt little in common with unionised industrial workers but the 7th Btn would also have included some men from the mining areas around Methil who might have had more sympathy. Perhaps the awareness of being in the trenches versus those safe at home homogenised group identity. Or perhaps those who felt some sympathy would think better of expressing their opinion in the hearing of someone like Maxwell whose views would be only too well known.

That is not to say that Maxwell thought the men under his command were above reproach and in what may be thought to be a somewhat unfeeling remark given the local deaths which had relatively recently occurred he told the local press, "I would like to emphasise that the dangers of trench work are very much over-estimated by relatives at home. We have long spells in the trenches with few or no casualties, and in many cases casualties that have occurred have been due to the carelessness of the soldiers themselves in not exercising proper caution."[58] However it may be that in his brusque way he was actually trying to provide reassurance.

Whatever the strains on the men or their relatives, the effect of the war on him was debilitating and by the end of September 1915 it was reported

---

[55] EoFR 15 July 1915

[56] EoFR 30 September 1915

[57] Of this strike it has been observed " the most militant workers were often also the most patriotic - South Wales and Clydeside the two centres of industrial discontent also provided the highest proportion in the country of recruits for the army. But the workers were unwilling to sacrifice their rights or to work overtime, if this brought increased profits to their employers as it inevitably did." Taylor p 39

[58] EoFR 30 September 1915

that the "the strain the gallant officer has undergone has necessitated a rest and he is at present in hospital." He never really recovered sufficiently to go back to active service. Towards the end of 1915 he was in Anstruther and even attended a meeting of the town council in his old capacity as Town Clerk (confirming the stereotype that Kitchener had of the Territorials being a Town Clerks' army.[59]) In January he was back on military duty and was soon to be appointed Military representative for the tribunals for Fife and Kinross. (These Tribunals heard applications for exemptions or postponements to the call up after the introduction of conscription.)

He and his wife remained prominent in the town throughout the war suffering their own family sadness when on 30 August 1917 she delivered a still-born child at their home Blair Lodge. In June 1918 Major Maxwell was awarded the OBE for his military services.

His prominence in local reports of the war can be attributed more to his status in the local community than to his military exploits. (When he was home on sick leave a reporter was despatched to interview him - the account appearing with the underwhelming headline - " Interesting talk with Captain Maxwell"). It may also be due to the likelihood that he was a more frequent or detailed correspondent home than his men and that extracts from his letters formed the basis for the admiring reports.

Whilst the 7th Battalion Black Watch was the local pre-war territorial battalion the 8th drew on those who had joined the colours after the outbreak of war. Its "rank and file came mainly from city offices, from the plough and from the Fife Collieries."[60] It was formed as a unit in the 26th (Highland) Brigade of the 9th (Scottish) Division of Kitchener's New Army. Despite not having evenings of drill and annual camps to prepare the men for conflict the 8th was sent to France within days of the Territorials and was blooded in the front line at Festubert just as the 7th had been.

But neither their training or first taste of frontline experience could prepare them for what was to come. In September 1915 the 8th were given the objective of taking Loos.

The Germans were well prepared for what was an obviously impending allied offensive. They had reinforced their defences so that they were

---

[59] Wood p104
[60] Wauchope Vol 3 p 3

three miles deep in places, making it more difficult for the bombardment which preceded the attack to have an impact. (In any case it seems the artillery fire was not only ineffectual but at times calamitous. A Fife artillery man who took part in the battle recalls that the old 15 pound guns they had to use lacked the range and the shells were falling short, killing men in the British trenches.)[61]

If that was not bad enough the British troops had also to cope with being gassed. Gas had been used on the eastern front by the Germans at the beginning of 1915 but that was a form of tear gas designed to incapacitate but not kill. However by April 1915 they had developed a chlorine based compound which was used at Ypres to terrifying effect. However it was an unpredictable weapon - depending on the wind to carry it on to the enemy.

The 8th battalion Black Watch was involved in the first ever use of gas by the British in battle at Loos. Even before the offensive had begun the men were dog tired with having carried the gas cylinders to the front. Great secrecy was attached to the deployment of the weapon which was described as 'the accessory' in Divisional orders.[62]

If commanders thought that it was going to be decisive in achieving a breakthrough they were mistaken. Firstly there were not sufficient gas canisters stockpiled to envelop the defensive trenches - when it was released at 5.50 am on the 25 September it was done so intermittently as there was not enough to permit continuous discharge for the 40 minutes leading up to the assault. Instead smoke candles were released in between to give the impression of gas cloud. Secondly the gas did not conveniently sweep across the German lines ahead of the British attack - instead it "hung around no man's land or even drifted back into the British trenches hindering rather than helping the advance."[63]

So after being bombarded by their own artillery, gassed by their own side and without sleep from the preparation for assault the 8th Black Watch were pitched over the parapets of their trenches and into the maelstrom of the German defensive machine gun fire. This was the battle in which it was said the German gunners eventually stopped firing at the retreating British forces, so sickened were they by the slaughter. It defies our understanding that men could walk into such a wall of death.

---

[61] MacDougall p92
[62] Wauchope Vol3 p9
[63] Keegan p218

One wounded local soldier William Mather tried to explain that although he and his colleagues were almost stunned by the continuous din of the artillery fire "the rush forward was carried out by men nerved up to the pitch to do anything required". He questioned if any of the Black Watch was "conscious of anything else but to get across the bullet swept space that divided them from the Germans."[64]

Two young Anstruther gardeners were lost on that first day's attack. Corporal John Louden a bright 22 year old died on the barbed wire, his body, it was reported, (sparing his parents no pain) riddled with bullets.[65] Private Hogg fell somewhere in the battle, a comrade writing home saying that it was only after 3 days of fierce fighting when a roll call was unanswered by Hogg that it was realised he had been lost.[66]

Corporal John Louden,
died on the barbed war during the Battle of Loos.

In the face of carnage the 8th actually captured the German lines despite the battle conditions being compounded by heavy rain and the Germans opening a sluice to flood the communication trench which led from their front lines to the secondary positions. As the 8th was moving amongst the buildings of Loos they were raked by bullets from enemy soldiers

[64] EoFR 21 Oct 1915
[65] EoFR 4 May 1916?
[66] EoFR 14 Oct 1915

firing from a school and Private William Pringle was shot through the head and, it was reported, died instantaneously.[67] Small comfort to his father who ran the well known ironmongers Gray and Pringle in Anstruther,[68] in which his son had worked alongside him.

In all the 8th Battalion Black Watch lost 19 officers and 492 other ranks in 3 days fighting. The British lost 16,000 killed and 25,000 wounded at Loos. According to one historian although the "battle had been a terrible and frustrating initiation to combat for the soldiers of the New Armies...the Scots of the 9th and 15th Divisions, in particular, seem to have shrugged off the casualties and taken setback as a stimulus to renewed aggression." [69] The account of the battle from another young Anstruther man, Philip Ray, fighting with the Cameronians gives some anecdotal encouragement to such a view. "Loos was in our hands in an hour or two but the attacking troops did not wait to clear it of Germans. Instead they pushed on and the bombers searched the village. Germans were found all over the place in houses, dug outs, cellars and those who were not taken prisoner were soon put out of our way by bombs. Everything went well until we got so far as Hill 70, the German third line, but here a warm time awaited us... the Germans had secured reinforcements and we were soon under a terrible hail of rifle and machine gun bullets varied by a dose of shrapnel. The order came to retire and reluctantly we did so. Three times we rallied and advanced but could not hold the Hill without supports. Just as we rallied for the third time another Division came up and thus we were able to hold what we had won."

This minster's son seems to have become a hardened soldier: "What I thought would trouble me most was the wounded but although I saw awful sights they had little effect on me. A large number of my "pals" have not returned but I can say no more about casualties at present. In due time you will see the lists."[70]

But if the casualties were being shrugged off at the front, at home it was a different matter. Loos cast a pall over the whole of the recruiting area for the Black Watch. So bad were the casualties it was said that next of kin were not informed immediately for fear of the effect on civilian morale of whole communities getting such news all at the same time.

[67] EoFR 7 Oct 1915
[68] The ironmongery shop is still operating to this day
[69] Keegan p218
[70] EoFR 14 Oct 1915

44

It was Loos which fostered the notion that "Scotland is small enough to know all her sons by heart"[71] built on a sense that everyone had lost a relative or a neighbour.

The last of Anstruther's sons to die in 1915 was Captain James Hay of the Seaforth Highlanders. He was in many ways the embodiment of an army which was formed not through compulsion but through a sense of patriotism and duty. He had no need to be in France at all. For a start he was 40 years old when the war broke out, married and living in Liverpool. True he had once been a regular soldier. The story romantically was told that as a 16 year old he had left on his desk in the office of Mr Cook (the tennis playing solicitor in Anstruther) the drawing of a soldier in full Highland uniform and went off to join the army. He was in uniform himself for 21 years seeing service in India, the Sudan and the Boer war before retiring and taking up a post with Jacob's Biscuits. Yet in 1914 he sought out his old regiment and re-enlisted.

He was given a commission having been a warrant officer previously. Under the headline 'Risen from the Ranks' the local paper tartly observed that "the only surprising feature is that he was not promoted to the commissioned ranks many years ago."[72] Lieutenant Hay was sent to Fort George to be the Adjutant of the 9th battalion, Seaforth Highlanders which was to become the first Pioneer battalion of the British Army and the first to land in France.[73] Pioneers were formed when it was realised that the demands of trench warfare required logistical efforts which outstripped the capacity of the Royal Engineers. So Pioneers "made miles of roads and communications trenches; made strong points; joined our sapheads to those of the enemy in attack; made strong dug outs and emplacements for trench mortars; and dealt with trench draining, field tramways."[74]

Hay went with the battalion to France on May 9th 1915. However the strains of war saw him, by the summer, invalided at an infantry base depot, and on his recovery he was offered the post of Adjutant of Number 15 Base Depot which would have kept him out of the firing line. However as he explained to a relative in a letter home, "I told the Colonel who kindly offered the appointment that so long as I was fit for the fighting

---

[71] Hay p47

[72] EoFR 17 December 1914

[73] MacEachern p421

[74] MacEachern p427

45

line I scarcely thought it right that I should occupy a nice comfortable billet at the base."[75] Instead he was given the task of getting reinforcements up the line to the front and was proud of his men for standing up to artillery fire which was shelling the station as they formed up on the platform. Having got them to safety he went off with three subalterns to look for some place to eat. "The only thing we could get was a cafe below ground and eventually got served with coffee, eggs and stale bread for which we had to pay 4s 2d. The inhabitants of the town were all living in cellars and the proprietor of the cafe took us to another cellar further along the street. The dampness of the place rather appalled us so we got a candle and explored upstairs. Signs of hasty flight were everywhere."[76]

Here, still behind the frontline he paints an almost bucolic picture of the Scottish soldier invoking their rural heritage. "Our men are on very good terms with the French people in this district, especially the peasant class. You can see the British soldiers working in the fields at night helping to hoe potatoes, their turnips or bind sheaves of wheat and barley. The other night I came across a stalwart lad of the Black Watch wielding a huge scythe most skilfully in a corn field greatly to the admiration of two French reapers he was helping."[77]

Captain James Hay

---

[75] EoFR 29 July 1915

[76] ibid

[77] ibid

But these men were shortly to go through the hellfire of Loos. Hay was attached to the 8th Battalion Seaforths which fought alongside Hogg, Louden and Pringle's Black Watch and Ray's Cameronians. Hay himself however died in November 1915 when according to one battalion commentator they had " settled down to the dreary life of trench warfare"[78] He had been killed in a war which he could have avoided, could have left and could have kept out of harm's way. He was soon to be replaced by soldiers who would fight but only because they had been obliged to do so.

---

[78] Sym p172

Chapter 4

1916 - No choice but to fight

Until 1916 the war had been fought by what was, effectively, a volunteer army. Even after almost a year and a half of conflict, when new recruits must have been fully aware of the conditions and risk into which they would be thrust, volunteers were still coming forward. However the attrition rate and the scale of conflict were such that this was not enough to meet the military commanders demands. There was also a degree of popular insistence that the risks should be borne equally not just by the brave but also the reluctant (or the 'shirkers').

In January 1916 the Military Act was passed. In the month or so before it was due to come into force an effort was made to squeeze more volunteers with the distribution of posters around Fife announcing 'Single Men! Will You March Too or Wait till March 2'. (Conscription initially applied to single men aged 18-41.)

The local paper heartily approved of this, and whilst it felt that there would be very few men in the district to whom the Act would actually apply, it was confident that the prospect of conscription would encourage the last remaining eligible men to come forward so that it could be said that all who served did so voluntarily. This confidence was misplaced and within days of the Act coming into force there was a local dispute over claims for exemption.

The Military Act provided grounds for exemptions to conscription. Those who suffered ill health, were engaged in work which was judged to be of national importance or were the sole breadwinner with dependants could apply for exemption. These cases were heard locally at military and medical tribunals. (Fishermen were also exempt from conscription into the army, as they were now to be regarded as a reserve for the Navy.)

When Andrew Brodie a local blacksmith claimed for exemption the military objected. He worked in his father's business - and his father happened to be Baillie Brodie a prominent local councillor and businessman. Baillie Brodie argued that his business could not remain open if all his staff were taken to war and that already nine men had enlisted from the shop. Furthermore he was angered by the call-up of Andrew when his son Thomas, who also worked as a blacksmith in the same shop, had already successfully gained a three month exemption.

The trouble was that the main business of the smithy was making golf clubs, but Provost Black argued on behalf of his friend that "it matters very little whether they make horse shoes or golf clubs none of the lads can be spared. It is the only little industry the burgh has. You would just as well put a shell into it as take these men away."

The East Neuk felt itself to be perpetually economically fragile given the cyclical fortunes of fishing and farming. Diversification into other industries like golf club making was important and when Baillie Brodie's cleek factory was opened in Anstruther Wester in January 1913 it was big news. An impressive ceremony was conducted at the laying of the foundation stone, under which a time capsule was buried consisting of a reputedly 500 year old urn (the property of Provost Porter) containing copies of the *The Scotsman, Dundee Advertiser, East of Fife Record, Daily Mail, Dundee Courier*, the list of voters and abstract of the Burgh accounts. The personal investment of the Baillie was acknowledged as a list of the Brodie family members was included in the urn. The factory would employ 15- 20 men which was important as "the want of labour has long been felt in this district."[79]

After Provost Black's impassioned speech, and despite the objections of the military, exemption was granted. This drew caustic comment in the letters pages of the *East of Fife Record* which without naming Brodie directly suggested that the Tribunals were easily persuaded that "golf cleek manufacture was one of these industries without which Britain's export trade would dwindle to vanishing point." As a result of leniency by tribunals, whose actions the writer claimed would not stand up to critical examination, "able bodied shirkers are being allowed to skulk behind the flimsiest excuse."[80]

There is little to suggest that the local tribunal regarded those claiming exemption as being shirkers - they clearly knew individual and local circumstances and were sympathetic, for example, to those whose businesses might fail. However the issue was that those in business in Anstruther and Cellardyke were often also those who sought public office by election to the Town Council, and local tribunals included local councillors. It is not difficult to see why this gave rise to suggestions of cronyism, even if not merited. Councillor Brodie was not an isolated case.

---

[79] EoFR 2 January 1913

[80] Letter EoFR 23 March 1916

Less than a year after Willie Watson's death his brother Robert was called up for active service. He was a married man but that was no longer grounds for exemption as the Military Act had not secured the expected number of single men, falling some 87,000 short of the 194,000 men anticipated. So the call up was extended to married men in May 1916. Still he claimed exemption and had a perfectly valid case. He had three young children after all, and the oilskin factory was contributing to the war effort. Oilskins had in the 19th century been produced by hand by the wives of fishermen. It was laborious process in which hand stitched cotton cloth garments were hand coated with linseed oil and dried in cellars or garrets. Each oilskin needed four coats and each coat need up to five weeks to dry. Watson's had not only mechanised the process but had built new proofing towers 80 ft high allowing lighter fabrics to be treated. The firm had to meet the demands of the navy which required the crews of submarine patrol boats and minesweepers to be kitted out. In addition to oilskins the firm made buoys. Robert was represented at the tribunal by his father's junior partner Mr Mitchell. He successfully argued that the firm had already four men enlisted, two of whom (including Willie Watson) had been killed.[81]

You could see why there might be local grumbling about connections. As previously mentioned, the tribunal included councillors and Mitchell was a local councillor; the military representative on the Fife and Kinross Tribunals with the responsibility of challenging what was regarded as unjustified claims for exemption was Captain Maxwell who was the Council's Town Clerk. The tribunal was being asked to decide on the claim by a prominent local business man whom Maxwell knew well. He had been Willie Watson's Commanding Officer and had seen him killed. He must also have known Robert Watson. As a married man Robert did not live at the family home at 'Craigholm' but at 2 St Ayles Crescent. According to the 7th Battalion Diary and Almanack, which provided the officers' addresses Maxwell had lived at St Ayles Crescent too. Yet inescapably Robert did have a justified claim to be excused from conscription. Furthermore exemption was being sought for all the men in the factory who were called up.

In the meantime the letters of condolence and telegrams were coming in for other local men who had gone to the front. Generally bad news came home relatively swiftly. Sapper Andrew Black who had been a miner in west Fife was killed by the explosion of a German mine on 20 February and the news was in the local press a fortnight later. In the

---

[81] EoFR 13 April 1916

majority of cases acknowledgement in the Death notices of the local press was within three weeks. Sometimes however news would come not from official sources but in letters home from colleagues especially when a man had gone missing. Sometimes it could come in a brutal fashion from military sources. Sergeant George Wilson had like many before him served his time as plumber/ tinsmith with Gray and Pringles before emigrating to Canada where he volunteered with the 31st Battalion of the Canadian Infantry (Alberta Regiment) The first that Sophia Wilson knew of the fate of her 26 year old son was when a letter she had sent to him was returned to her home in Shore Street, Cellardyke by the Post Office with the bald intimation "Killed in action. Location unknown"[82] [83]

Sergeant George Wilson
'Killed in action; location unknown'

Whilst there was a steady stream of bad news from the trenches, little was being heard from the Navy. No Anstruther man had been lost from a warship since the battle of Coronel. For months the German's High Seas Fleets had largely been confined to port making darting raids out to bombard the English coast and then back to the safety of harbour

---

[82] EoFR 27 April 1916

[83] (His father John was the fisherman who had in 1915 been admonished despite contravening the fishing restrictions on account of having three sons on active service. One of those other sons, 33 year old David, had gone off on drifter patrol on the local boat the *Coreopsis* and was later to be lost at sea in October 1917. Yet despite living locally with his wife he is not recorded on the Cellardyke memorial).

before the British could respond. At the end of May 1916 however Admiral Jellicoe commander of the British Grand Fleet was alerted that the vast bulk of the German fleet was in open water in the North Sea. The British response of sending its battle fleet from Rosyth and Scapa Flow meant that 250 ships converged off the coast of Denmark. Never before had so many or such powerful ships gathered to do battle. On board *HMS Invincible*, the flagship of the 3rd Battle cruiser squadron, was Stoker James Moncrieff. The 22 year old from West Forth Street in Cellardyke had been an engineer on the fishing boat *Vanguard III* and was one of the first to enlist. He had already seen action in the Battle of the Falklands when the *Invincible* had avenged the loss of the *Monmouth* and *Good Hope* at Coronel by sinking the *Gneisenau* and *Scharnhorst*.

If the British expected the Jutland encounter to be a latter day Trafalgar they were mistaken. As each side pounded the other in the confused conditions caused by mist and smoke - " smoke from burning ships, smoke from funnels, smoke from gun muzzles and smoke deliberately created to conceal and preserve"[84] - the German ships seemed better able to take punishment. The British suffered some catastrophic losses, prompting Admiral Beatty to famously say, "There is something wrong with our bloody ships today."[85] There was certainly something wrong with the *Invincible*. At 6.30pm the battle cruiser had launched a powerful attack on the Germans and its crew were being praised for the excellence of their gunnery (which they had been practising off Scapa Flow) when a German shell smashed through the 7 inch armour of one of *Invincible's* gun turrets and set off an explosive chain reaction which blew up its magazines and tore the ship in half. So shallow were the waters that the bow and stern both stood high out of the waves. The *Invincible* sank with the loss of 1,026 men - Stoker Moncrieff was not amongst the six survivors.

In all the Royal Navy lost over 6,000 sailors at Jutland. The Germans with losses of 2,500 felt justified in calling it the Victory of Skaagerak. The British however claimed strategic success on the grounds that the German fleet had sustained damage on such a scale that it would take six months to become a fighting force again and was for the rest of the war largely confined to port and coastal waters.

On dry(ish) land, just as the volunteers were beginning to get to the front the Regulars were still fighting on. In the enthusiastic rush to the colours

---

[84] Hough p249
[85] Halpern p319

it is easy to overlook the fact that in peacetime the British army had been over 11,000 men short and Regulars were not held in high esteem by society. Ordinary soldiers according to one historian tended to be "vagabonds who could find no better occupation; recruits from the bars and brothels of urban slums or the human detritus thrown up by the shrinkage of agricultural Britain."[86]

If this was how Regular soldiers were viewed, spare a thought then for Private David Bell of the 2nd Battalion Black Watch. A veteran of the Boer War, at 41 and married he might have avoided conscription if he had been at home in a civilian occupation. Instead after a year on the western front during which 350 of his comrades had been killed, he celebrated Hogmanay 1915 in Basra, the day his troop ship *Royal George* docked nearly a month after steaming out of Marseille.

They were immediately transported onto paddle steamers and sent up the Tigris river to try to relieve the 12,000 men of the British Expeditionary Force, surrounded by the Turks at Kut al-amara. In all there were four assaults to try to lift the siege. Private Bell survived the first two even though they shattered the 2nd battalion to such an extent that it was forced to reform as a Highland battalion with the remnants of the Seaforth Highlanders.

At 7 am on 22 April 1916 with 20 years of apparently little regarded service to the colours behind him Bell began what was for him and the Black Watch the final assault. It was a shambles. The British guns had only enough ammunition for a 35 minute bombardment so machine guns were called into action to augment the artillery fire. When the Highlanders massed on the narrow 300 yard front on which the attack was to take place they found themselves being shot at from their own machine guns and were forced to throw themselves into the four inches of water covering the ground, to avoid being killed by their own side. Floundering through the mud they tried to get to grips with the Turks but were unable to maintain the attack in trenches deep in water, as they ran out of grenades and the majority of rifles became so clogged with mud that they could not be fired. So died Private Bell, husband, father of five and Regular soldier.

Back in France another old soldier who didn't fade away but died, was Sergeant John C Wood of the Seaforths. He had been one of the first to bring back to the East Neuk the reality of war, after being wounded

---

[86] DeGroot p14

in the early weeks. A former chauffeur to Colonel Erskine at Grangemuir outside Pittenweem he had landed in France less than three weeks after the outbreak of war. The story which Wood could tell was not glorious. After losing 17 men killed in bombardment the 2nd found itself supposedly acting as rearguard to a British 4th division but in reality having no idea where the division actually was. A forced march, still wearing greatcoats under an August sun and without food and water set the tone for a ten day retreat in which the footsore men covered 134 miles.

By the following month however the war had taken on its characteristic of trench warfare when the Germans dug in at the River Aisne. Wood was amongst the Seaforths who confronted them in mid September, crossing the river at midnight on a single remaining girder of a blown bridge, before he was wounded. He was invalided back to Scotland first to Stobhill hospital in Glasgow and then to a friend's house in Anstruther where he could be found still wearing his blood stained uniform and coming to terms with the news that his brother had been killed in the same battle.[87] A shrapnel wound and a sore heart did not keep you out of the war and he was back in action fighting at Mons, and was mentioned in despatches in May 1916. His number was up though and the following month he was killed in action. His burial along with thirteen other Seaforth Highlanders was the first to take place at what became Mailly Wood cemetery.

For Sergeant Wood's mother at home in Dunfermline losing more than one son in the war was a tragedy but one which she shared with many mothers. The curtains were pulled more than once in several homes in Anstruther and Cellardyke. As far as can be established there are eight sets of brothers on the two local memorials. There's the Canadian gunner WL Cairns and his Army Service Corps brother James Cairns; Black Watch Private Andrew Dick and his brother Naval Reservist James Dick; fisherman turned Signaller Hugh Dickson and Black Watch Private William Dickson. There are two lots of Moncrieffs - Gordon Highlander George Moncrieff and Seaforth Highlander James Moncrieff, and then there was Royal Scot William Moncrieff who had survived the Gretna rail crash, and his brother Alex who joined up in Canada. Twenty year old vanman Robert Parker died of his wounds fighting with the Black Watch whilst his brother William Parker of the London Postal Rifles died in a London hospital, never having reached the battlefield. The

---

[87] CBO 1 October 1914 His brother was Sergeant Major Wood 1st Battalion Cameron Highlanders, killed in the Battle of the Aisne on 14 September 1914. 33 years old, he lived at Lady Lawson Street in Edinburgh. He is not commemorated on either of the Anstruther/ Cellardyke memorials.

posthumously decorated Black Watch regular Thomas Swan was killed in the first year of the war aged 26; his younger brother William died in the last year of the war at the same age. Finally there was James and David Watt both coopers to trade and both Black Watch.

(Many more local men than this lost brothers. For instance John Wood's brother is not on the memorials; nor mystifyingly is George Wilson's brother David who was lost from a local boat on patrol duties.)

Perhaps the most poignant of those who are listed are the Archibald brothers. William and Robert joined up with the Royal Scots famous 16th battalion which had been cheered the length of Princes Street as the men marched, on 16 June 1915, to Waverley station en route to war. The battalion had been formed by Sir George McCrae who, after only 13 days, had attracted 1,350 men "from all classes; students, artisans, clerks and a phalanx of footballers."[88] At the head of the ranks were indeed the Heart of Midlothian professional footballers whose recruitment had attracted so much attention. McCrae was the owner of a drapery business.[89] By coincidence Robert Bruce Archibald, father of the new recruits, was also a successful businessman in the clothing industry having been a tweed manufacturer in Tillicoultry before going off to the West Indies. The Royal Scots Edinburgh City battalions were not entirely comprised of the capital's citizens. There had been an attempt for instance to form a Manchester Scottish battalion but when recognition was refused many of the 300 who had enlisted travelled up to join Edinburgh City 1st battalion which became the 15th Royal Scots.[90] Robert Archibald was married and living in Twickenham when he joined the 16th.

A year later the brothers were part of a mass of men being gathered for a major assault on the Somme. The British forces had been swollen by the Kitchener New Army recruits to now stand at more than 10 times its normal peacetime size. War had become a matter of logistics in the deployment of men, accumulation of materiel, and construction of communications infrastructure. But at the end of the day (or rather at the beginning of the day when attacks invariably took place) it was still about a hastily trained, overburdened citizen soldier being prepared to step over a parapet and face the prospect of death or maiming. As John Keegan has said "the simple truth of 1914-18 trench warfare is that the massing of large numbers of soldiers unprotected by anything but cloth

---

[88] Ewing p10
[89] Wood p103
[90] Middlebrook p12

uniforms however they were trained, however they were equipped against large masses of other soldiers protected by earthworks and barbed wire and provided with rapid fire weapons was bound to result in very heavy casualties among the attackers."

This is not a matter of hindsight. It was known, of course, to the military commanders of the time and the British preparations for the battle of the Somme were intended to minimise if not indeed eliminate the advantage of the German defenders. The plan was for the greatest artillery barrage in military history to precede the assault with the intention of sweeping away the barbed wire and pulverising the defensive positions; any soldiers who survived would be kept stunned and cowering in their dugouts by a creeping barrage from field guns which would lift in time for the attacking forces in overwhelming and irresistible numbers not just to take frontline positions but, according to General Haig, to breakthrough all German lines to take the village of Bapaume more than seven miles from the British starting point.

That was the intention. The reality was different. Certainly the barrage was stunning - it opened on 24 June and the Germans were bombarded each morning for 80 minutes. 1,437 British guns fired 1,508,652 shells at a cost of £6 million.[91] But these statistics belie the effectiveness of the weaponry. The British (and the French) had the wrong guns for the job. Against entrenched positions with the soldiers sheltering in dugouts a gun with a high trajectory was required to fire a shell with high explosive which, dropping down onto the trenches, had a chance of penetrating the defences. Instead the British relied upon old guns which fired too small a shell at too flat a trajectory to cause sufficient damage. If that was not bad enough the quality and choice of shell negated the expected effect of the numbers actually fired. Three out of four shells sent over were shrapnel, in the mistaken belief that this would cut the barbed wire. As for the high explosives almost one third of them failed to explode.[92]

As a result barbed wire was thrown in the air and resettled often in even denser clumps; the Germans did cower in their dugouts but survived in far greater numbers than allowed for. Yet the awe inspiring effect of the bombardment convinced the British commander General Rawlinson that the normal tactics of frontal assault could be overturned. Instead of a dawn attack zero hour was to be 7.30 am when it had been light for over three hours; instead of the men crawling out into No Man's Land under

<hr>

[91] Middlebrook p105

[92] Mosier p234

cover of darkness and behind a creeping barrage the British forces were expected to walk across in broad daylight. The barrage was to be lifted 15 minutes before zero hour to give them free passage, believing that the Germans would remain in their dugouts still expecting a full 80 minutes of shelling as had been the pattern for the previous week.

On that morning of the attack 1st July 1916, Robert and William Archibald would have been adjusting their equipment, awed if not stunned themselves as the "cannonade swelled in volume and the earth shook under the frenzied roar, the eastern sky became a sheet of light and flame in which puffs of bursting shrapnel formed a variety of distorted arabesques."[93] At 7.15 the bombardment lifted and at 7.28 two huge mines were exploded throwing earth 4,000 feet into the air. One Royal Scot felt that "the whole world seemed to be moving: the earth moved sideways and back three times before the final explosion of the mine. At 7.30[94] the brothers Lance Corporal William and Private Robert Archibald stepped out into the battle of the Somme and into the maelstrom of death. The Germans had survived in sufficient numbers and with their wits about them to realise that the explosion of the mines heralded an attack. With the British forces queuing up to walk across No Man's Land, and probing for a way through the still intact defensive wires there was time enough to set up machine guns. One Highlander witnessed the result: "I could see that our leading waves had got caught by their kilts. They were killed hanging on the wire, riddled with bullets like crows shot on a dyke." The Archibalds died that morning, the only Anstruther commemorated brothers to die in the same battalion, in the same attack. In all the British lost 20,000 men killed, 35,000 wounded and only 585 taken prisoner. Almost half of the men who attacked that day became casualties; as did 75% of the officers.[95]

Attention has been focussed on that first day (when Anstruther also lost Lance Corporal John Moncrieff. The 28 year old Seaforth Highlander whose family home was at George Street had been an apprentice cooper with the well known local firm Melville and Co before going to South Shields.). The scale of the losses on 20 July might have caused the resolve of commanders and troops to falter. It was not that death by the thousands had not been experienced - it was that death in so many

---

[93] Ewing p271

[94] A Royal Scots historian says that at 7.30 the first waves of the 15 Btn climbed the parapets and advanced into No Man's Land (Ewing p271). According to one participant they were already out in No Man's Land waiting, when the mines went off at 7.28 (Cpl H Beaumont MM in Middlebrook p124)

[95] Middlebrook p263

thousands had never before been experienced and given that the commanders had sought to persuade their men if not indeed themselves that the assault would be a literal walkover then its impact might have been even more undermining.

The Somme has been the focus of heated debate about the quality of British decision making. The Somme itself and the ostensible target Bapaume (pop. 3,000, now twinned with Anstruther) was of no military import and seems to have been chosen by Haig on the grounds that it was where the French and British forces abutted each other. You could argue that the commanders were forced to use the guns that were available but then perhaps they should not have presumed they would be effective as their deficiencies must have been known by then. But there was no requirement to make men walk across the battlefield heavily laden with kit and equipment. The French had abandoned this approach and at the Somme their men, clustered in platoons, ran forward taking advantage of what cover they could. As a consequence their casualty numbers were significantly less than the British.

Yet it would appear that the generals had come to the accept that "the basic stark fact was that the conditions of trench warfare between 1914-18 predisposed to slaughter."[96] Undeterred by the first day losses the battle of the Somme went on for months, closing officially on 19th November - by which time British losses amounted to 420,000 killed and wounded.

Casualty numbers en masse and on that scale defy comprehension. But they were made up of a tithe from towns and villages throughout Britain, each one an individual loss. Anstruther's contribution was a further seven men accounting in total for almost 10% of all local losses in the First World War.

Gone was Davie Watt - another of Anstruther's coopers who had fought and been wounded at Loos. His 8th battalion Black Watch was so badly depleted by the German shelling and counter attack at Longueval that eight reserve officers and all available NCO's and men were sent up from the transport lines as reinforcements. However on the night of the 17th July "the Battalion transport and ration parties were caught up in a barrage of high explosive and gas shells and suffered many casualties among both personnel and animals."[97]

---

[96] Keegan p316
[97] Wauchope Vol3 p24

Before July 1916 was out another of Anstruther's favoured sons was killed. George Cunningham was one of those men who should have been the future of the town. At 28 he was not a boy and already well known about the place. He was making his contribution to local civic society as Secretary of the YMCA and Treasurer of Gospel Temperance Union. He worked with his father who was a prominent ships chandler and who would go on to become the Town Provost. (In years to come his brother Alex, who won a Military Medal in the Royal Army Medical Corps, would return to take on the family business which operated out of the yards which now form the courtyard of the Scottish Fisheries Museum).

George sent cheery and thoughtful messages back home - thanking the ladies of the Comforts Committee for sending across a batch of candles for local lads and letting them know that as daylight did not penetrate their deep dugouts the gift was much appreciated.[98] The manner of his death on 31 July 1916 was not as a warrior but in a moment of self sacrifice, cut down as he was tending the wounds of a Pittenweem soldier.

George Cunningham was Willie Watson's good friend and had been the witness to his will before the 1/7 Black Watch left Kinghorn. Their family homes faced each other over present-day Bankie Park. This friendship was well known and the local press was moved to note when reporting George's death that "He is another of the best of our young men who have made the supreme sacrifice and it is pathetic to look on a photograph in which Cunningham, Watson and Pringle are depicted, all of whom now sleep their last sleep in regions devastated by war."[99]

Lost too was Captain HR Lindsay the English teacher at Waid Academy. His family home was in Bolton and he joined the Loyal Northern Lancashire Regiment. He had come to the school in 1912, a graduate of Manchester University and made an immediate impact especially in devising the House System for sports which continued for decades thereafter. When war broke out, instead of returning for the new term, he joined up. He did send an apologetic note to the Rector saying he was sorry for the trouble he was causing by enlisting but explaining simply that "it seemed the only thing to do." Notwithstanding his brief teaching career the board of Governors fully supported his patriotic decision and agreed that not only would they keep his place open for him, they would also pay him the difference between his army pay (£95:13:3d per annum) and his teachers pay of £150. In January 1916 the school's flag was

---

[98] EoFR18 May 1916

[99] EoFR 10 August 1916

hoist in his honour when he was awarded the Military Cross. The following month he was back on leave and went up to the school to spend a 'social hour' with the senior pupils. The school magazine records how enthralled they were by Captain Lindsay's description of the "worst scrap he had ever been in". He told the rapt pupils of how a Lancashire's advance on enemy frontline was halted by barbed wire entanglements which the Artillery had failed to clear. The Germans had them pinned on three sides and lobbed bombs at them from side trenches which accounted for their last remaining machine gun. The situation was grave. Like a Boy's Own story to be continued in the next thrilling chapter Henry Lindsay did not tell them how they had escaped. This was assumed to be modesty on his part as it was surmised that he had volunteered to break out of the trap to summon reinforcements, for which action he won his MC. Following his death the school Governors let it be known that they had a claim against his estate in respect of contributions to the Superannuation Fund made while he was serving but "in the exceptional circumstances resolved to waive the claim."[100]

The Somme also claimed Thomas Drummond. He was with the Scots Guards 2nd battalion as it attacked at Ginchy on 15 September. The ground was pockmarked with shell holes from British bombardment and every landmark and distinguishing feature had been obliterated. Military intelligence had it that there were no intermediate trenches between them and their objective. In fact the shell holes had been connected up by the Germans and two lines of defences had to be overcome even before the Scots Guards reached the main German trench. The fighting was ferocious, with the Germans, it was said, defending their lines to the last man and causing heavy losses on the British side. The 2nd battalion which had been held back from the initial assault moved forward at 9 am but quickly came under shell fire. As the men advanced to dig in under cover of a hill ridge they were being picked off by rifle fire from wounded or stray Germans left behind in shell holes.[101]

It may be that one of these accounted for Thomas Drummond. He was known to have been wounded and was making his way back to a dressing station. He never made it - either he got lost or was ambushed. Amazingly, although his body was never found, his photograph and papers were later discovered on the body of a dead German.[102]

---

[100] EoFR 5 October 1916

[101] Petre et al p158

[102] EoFR 2 November 1916

It was somehow ironic that his possessions should be taken as he lost his life. The year previously he had written a touching letter to schoolchildren in Cellardyke who had used the proceeds of a school concert to buy "a strong serviceable knife to be sent to each soldier or sailor belonging to West Anstruther, East Anstruther, Cellardyke and Kilrenny with an inscription suitable to the occasion".[103]

Thomas Drummond's thank you note had said: "I scarcely know how to thank the bairns of your district for the splendid gift. I am very well pleased with it and hope to enjoy the use of it for a long time to come... I will never forget that gift wherever I go."[104] In 1917 the family of the ex locomotive fireman back home at Shore Road, West Anstruther learned he had been recommended for a Distinguished Conduct Medal.[105]

A month later one of Thomas Drummond's neighbours from Shore Road, young Robert Parker, was in the frontline with the 8th Battalion Black Watch. It was not Parker's first time at the Somme front as the 8th had been involved in an abortive attack in mid September and had spent most of the four days in the frontline recovering the corpses of Black Watch territorials. Parker, a vanman before joining up, had a couple of Cellardyke lads for company Alex Boyter (22) a plasterer from Rodger Street and Robert Sherrif (20) of George Street, a cleekmaker turned machine gunner. On the 19 October 1916 the Fife men were in Snag trench which had been captured the day before. They had spent a miserable night in pouring rain and were looking forward to day break. Dawn brought no relief - quite the opposite. At 5.30 am the waterlogged trench became a scene of mayhem as firstly South African troops tumbled into it retreating from a German counterattack, quickly followed by grenades of German bombers. Scarcely able to move because of the crush of bodies and in the appalling conditions the Black Watch suffered heavy casualties. Parker died of serious wounds sustained in the German charge. What happened to Sherrif was never known. His family had to suffer a year of painfully wondering after being told that their son was missing, wounded in action but heard nothing more until he was officially confirmed dead in October 1917. Alex Boyter died in a bombing raid as the Black Watch began a counteroffensive which retook the trench by noon making the 19 October 1916 as bad as the first day on the Somme so far as the local community was concerned.

---

[103] EoFR 11 March 1915

[104] EoFR 27 May 1915

[105] CBO 15 February 1917

For the Boyters however the whole war was grievous. Alex the plasterer was cousin to 25 year old Alex the ex plumber's apprentice (and latterly stoker on a drifter) who was killed earlier in the year by a German shell. Both Cellardyke boys came from a large and well known family. But theirs was not the only lost generation because both of these lads' fathers were also gone. The father of Alex Boyter (Bowman) had been a fisherman drowned at sea 16 years previously; the father of Alex Boyter (Brown) also a fisherman was blown up after hitting a German mine in the North Sea.

Even this late in the war the local connection between the officers, men and community was being maintained. Alex Boyter's family received news of his death from Philip Ray who was now a Lieutenant in the Black Watch. Towards the end of the year it was Colonel T D Murray of the 4th Battalion Black Watch, a prominent local solicitor and freemason in Anstruther, who wrote to the family of Private Angus McKay to say that their son had been in a charge and there was little hope that he was now alive. He had been with another local man who had lost him in the mist and darkness.

One notable feature of the report of 22 year old Private McKay's death was that he had been home to Kilrenny with trench fever in September but according to the local paper had "got over it."

The very fact that it was reported that McKay suffered from what is elsewhere called shellshock or neurasthenia and the sympathetic manner in which it is done seems to suggest that there was little stigma attached to it with no hint of cowardice or malingering. But then McKay, having got over it, had gone back to the front and died bravely charging the enemy. By contrast it is interesting that the term trench fever is not used in respect of Captain Maxwell or Captain Hay who we know were invalided as a result of what is more coyly termed 'the strain of war.' Given latter day estimates of the number of those who suffered to the extent of needing treatment, trench fever is probably underreported by the local press and there may have been a family unwillingness to offer up information as to why their son was home or in hospital. According to some estimates "behaviour disorder without physical cause" accounted for 9% of battle casualties and after the war 50,000 men were awarded pensions on mental grounds.[106]

Leaving aside those who were mentally unfit at the time of joining up,

---

[106] Winter D pp129-130

what was it that these men were suffering from and what had caused it? The suggestion is that the First World War represented the first conflict in which no man was safe and never felt out of danger. Deaths might be expected in battles - but it was the constant possibility of death whilst going about innocuous activities which strained the nerves. Take Hay's previously mentioned Pioneer battalion for instance - its job was not to go over the top or carry out trench raids. But as a consequence they found themselves in the frontline for longer than other troops. Even a contemporary notes without bravura "Pioneers were considered tireless and nerveless so when their own Division retired from the line they were lent to another... they were always under fire and seldom got rest through a sense of perfect safety." In the course of the war the 9th Battalion, ostensibly trench diggers, suffered 1,436 casualties.

The dangers which men faced were from gas and shrapnel, sudden trench raids, or underground mine explosions. The problem, then, according to

Private Alexander Watson, killed at the Somme

one commentator "was that in training no one had been prepared for vigilant inaction... for the demoralising stooped walk, for the need to take constant care."

The stooped walk was to avoid one of the real killers, sniper fire. The Germans had specialists, often staying in the same part of the Front for long periods of time. They worked in pairs - an observer to pick out targets and work out ranges, and then the sniper with his Mauser releasing a single shot. The result was perpetual and deadly danger since often it would be a head carelessly appearing above the parapet which would be the target. Certainly sniper fire accounted for several East Neuk men including the final two local men killed in 1916. Private Alexander Watson a 20 year old apprentice printer was shot whilst in the front line and for once the assurance to his widowed mother in James Street Cellardyke that her son died instantaneously may well have been correct. A few days after Christmas, Private John Smith another of Baillie Brodie's lads from the cleekmaking firm was shot by a sniper as he was making his way out of the trenches.

Chapter 5

The Home Front

How did more than two years of war affect daily life in Anstruther and Cellardyke? In obvious ways it was profound - for a fishing community to have its fishing restricted and many of its boats taken away from the harbour would have an observable effect. The comings and goings of the harbour on the tides; the reduction in fish landings and the knock-on economic effects on the coopers and processors would all observably change the character of the town, as well as affecting its income. The physical absence of the young men who had volunteered or were being called up would be noticeable. Some of the skippers who were fined for fishing beyond the limits argued that their boats were short-handed because so many men were away on naval service and that the old men who were left were less able to manage the boats.

The effect of war was also acknowledged to have some beneficial effects. Summer was made more enjoyable, it was felt, because of the introduction of British Summer Time stimulating an appreciation of the "lengthening out to bedtime of the days of August and the greater freshness of the early morning air."[107] The annual local water shortage was reportedly less pronounced in the summer of 1915 which was attributed to the population having decreased because of so many young fellows being away to war and because of the stoppage of the fishing industry which had consumed large quantities of water.

And the fishing stoppage also brought about an effective close time over the greater part of the North Sea. This would have been impossible to achieve under normal circumstances even though it was recognised that the ever increasing intensity of fishing operations was impoverishing the fishing grounds. The local paper was moved to consider the irony that "while men are seeking to destroy their kind, nature will see the chance to restock a zone which has been threatened by denudation."[108]

Whilst the war had a very direct effect on the fishing community, for many others in Anstruther and Cellardyke it was a case of adjusting to the circumstances of war whilst still going about daily business. You could tell there was a war on because of the restrictions on lighting although it was a long running sore that others were not so careful. An

---

[107] EoFR 7 September 1917
[108] EoFR 26 August 1915

editorial in the local paper complained that "North Berwick's lights are constantly in full use while towns on the northern coast are in darkness"[109] (Certainly the black out on the Fife side seems to have been effective. The skipper of the fishing boat *Midlothian* on its way home from North Shields lost his bearings coming into Anstruther on account of the darkness of the night and no lights showing at the harbour and eventually pitched ashore in a creek near Billowness to the west of the town.[110]) The editor returned to the issue almost two years later warning that the failure to darken lights "places the entire community in danger of being raided by enemy aeronauts."[111]

Fear of bombardment from the air far outstripped any real danger. But the Zeppelins literally brought the war home to the civilian population of Britain and their threat was magnified as a news-starved media reported at length on their appearance. The first Zeppelin appeared over the British coast at the very end of 1914 - and in total there were only 51 Zeppelin raids. London was bombarded in April 1915. All told 1,117 civilians were killed from aerial bombardments in the whole of the war, including from the more fearsome Gotha aeroplane bombers which actually made more sorties than the airships.[112] However the effect from the outset was dislocating with lighting restrictions and factories stopping work whenever a Zeppelin came into view. (Although ex Empress Eugenie claimed that when the Zeppelin was seen in January 1915 it occasioned no panic, observing that "the effect that these visits are having is no greater than that of a railway accident."[113]) Royal *sangfroid* aside, there was outrage at what was seen as tantamount to a war crime and proof of German barbarity. The East Fife local paper seemed to be in tune with the popular mood when it described the Zeppelin raids on Yarmouth and Scarborough as "simply organised murder of defenceless people" and demanded that there be no peace till provision was made for holding those responsible to account.

The raids may have provoked outrage but they also provided a marketing opportunity for the Perth based insurance company General Accident which began advertising its latest feature - Zeppelin risks.[114] How ironic

[109] CBO 22 October 1914

[110] EoFR 28 September 1916

[111] EoFR 31 August 1916

[112] Taylor p44

[113] Vansittart p54

[114] EoFR 30 September 1915

then that Perth Town Council complained of the spiralling cost of air raid insurance and when the premium reached nearly £73 in 1917 refused to pay.[115]

It was a widely held view that war was providing an opportunity for some to profit at others' misery. The *East of Fife Record* reported disapprovingly that "the profits of ship owners, millers and in fact all the leading firms engaged in food production more than doubled and trebled."[116] The paper was careful to make no mention of farm profits, the benefits of which might have been experienced rather closer to home. The need to feed an army and the reduction in food imports caused by German U boat activity saw farm profits in Britain increase five-fold between 1913 and 1917.[117] And as we have seen although fishing catches had fallen drastically, adding to the food shortage, the value of what was landed was often higher than the pre-war totals.

It was the differential ability to buy food that was the source of irritation. High wages were being earned in the munitions industries and elsewhere there was constant agitation by organised labour for wage increases to reflect the increased cost of living. But Anstruther had no munitions or military ancillary functions. The cost of basic necessities placed a strain on household budgets with a loaf of bread increasing by 40% between 1914-1916, meat, milk and butter doubling in price and sugar more than trebling. Even potatoes grew in price following a bad harvest.[118]

It was all the more commendable then that one of the constant features of wartime local life was the willingness of townsfolk to dip into their purses to support fund-raising initiatives to assist the war effort. There were constant concerts, fetes and operettas to raise money. The funds were divided between international relief for Belgian refugees and the work of the Red Cross on the one hand and benefits for local soldiers and sailors on the other.

Within a fortnight in early 1915 there were three events alone. The Picture House which operated out of the Town Hall devoted the whole of its proceeds (£12) of Monday 25 January to the Belgian Fund, the advert in the local press reminding potential patrons that "gallant little

---

[115] Harding p130
[116] EoFR 31 August 1916
[117] DeGroot p88
[118] DeGroot p 201

Belgium had barred the way to the match of the unscrupulous German forces."[119] The same cause was also supported by the Anstruther Philharmonic Society through its whist drive. Meanwhile a school concert by the pupils of Cellardyke Public School raised £25.8s.6d (after expenses) to send suitable gifts to "Oor Ain Folk in the Navy and Army".[120] (It was from the proceeds of this concert that a serviceable knife suitably inscribed was sent to each soldier and sailor from West Anstruther, East Anstruther Cellardyke and Kilrenny.)

Fundraising benefits were also used to give legitimacy to what might in the circumstances be seen as inappropriate activities. This was part of the adjustment of normal life to wartime conditions. So in November 1915 it was announced that a billiards competition was to be held in the Murray Library. Those entering were asked to make a contribution to the Red Cross as this, it was candidly admitted, would help "to take any stigma away from holding a tournament at the present time."[121]

At the end of that year a letter appeared in the local paper letting it be known that the crews of Cellardyke drifters on patrol duty had received money as reward for the sinking of a German submarine and they were donating £2 of it to buy something for the men at the front. But if there was any doubt that Anstruther and Cellardyke were separate communities, it is dispelled by the stipulation that "it has to be given only to the Cellardyke soldiers in the trenches."[122]

(Not all local people directed their donations through local collections. The womenfolk of the Jamieson family, 'Mansefield' Anstruther appear regularly in the lists of donors printed in *The Scotsman* giving generous donations of up to £3 each to Edinburgh appeals.)

Cellardyke naval men home on leave doubled their donation in August 1916 when they contributed to the proceeds of the Grand Fete held that summer which raised a staggering £503. It was reported that it took two men to carry the bag from the Academy to the Clydesdale Bank".[123] Reflecting the post-Somme reality of war the proceeds were destined for local disabled soldiers and sailors, the Scottish Blinded Soldiers and Sailors Fund and the Red Cross.

---

[119] EoFR 21 January 1915
[120] EoFR 28 January 1915
[121] EoFR 11 November 1915
[122] EoFR 9 December 1915
[123] EoFR 31 August 1916

There was to be no let up on the demands on local generosity. In February 1917 there were four events advertised: a grand operetta houp-la to provide comforts for local soldiers; (raised over £61 which was spent on 100 parcels of cigarettes, 184 shirts and 33 dozen handkerchiefs[124]); a concert by the Highland Cyclist Battalion Pierrot troupe specifically for HCB boys serving overseas (raised £15.12s.10d); a grand concert by Dundee Artistes to support local disabled soldiers and sailors; and a concert by the Leven Black and White Pierrot Entertainers in aid of Belgian relief funds. Admission for these events ranged from a top price of over 2/- down to 6d for children.

Red Cross collectors pose on the steps of Johnston Lodge

The most regular events however were fundraisers for the Sphagnum Moss Appeal. Local women throughout the war prepared dressings to be sent to field hospitals to treat the wounded. In March 1917 for example they responded to an appeal from the French Wounded Emergency Fund for regular supplies of moss to be used for stuffing pillows as hospitals had run out of head pillows and "pillows for lessening the pain of the wounded part." The Anstruther work party that month made up 139 pillows using waste moss. The dressings themselves were made from carefully picked moss, and funds were needed to pay for the large quantities of muslin bandaging involved.[125]

It was the role of the womenfolk of Anstruther and Cellardyke to organise

<hr />

[124] EoFR 25 October 1917

[125] EoFR 1 March 1917

these events; to decorate the halls; to get volunteers for the doors. The Red Cross volunteer collectors were exclusively women. They were organised by Georgina Murray, the wife of Col TD Murray and sister of George Darsie. Over 50 of them posed for a picture on the steps of Johnston Lodge, in their uniform and hats, collection trays at the ready. And of course it was women who made up the sphagnum moss work parties. We get to know very little of what happened to the local working girls in the war - what happened to them as the fishing catches fell; was there increased work on farms to compensate; did many go away to volunteer with the nursing and other services?

(Clearly not all of them were staying at home and doing good works. Private David Barclay of the Black Watch, who prior to joining up had been a fisherman living in John Street, Cellardyke brought a court action for divorce against his wife Cecilia on the grounds of infidelity. His sister in his absence told Sheriff Scott that her brother was married at Kinghorn in April 1915 and had left for the front the day after the marriage and did not see his wife again until December 1915. Yet she gave birth in May 1916. The court granted the petition and also gave permission for the register to be altered so that the child should be recorded as being illegitimate. As well as the stigma, the court ruling would have a serious affect on Cecilia Barclay's capacity to maintain herself. The wife of a private with one child received 15s at the beginning of the war which rose with inflation to 23s by the end. However allowances could be terminated on the grounds of infidelity or immoral behaviour.[126]

Individuals need not wait for a public subscriptions to get comforts to the front. Mungall the chemist in Pittenweem carried an extensive stock of soldier's comforts including " Anti thirst tablets - Bottle 6d; water steriliser tablets 1s; trench ointment in tubes 7 1/2d; and trench shirts impregnated with parasitic powder 1s.

Whether or not these items were of any real use they do indicate that civilians had some insight into the reality of conditions in the trenches. Soldiers were infested with lice which laid five eggs daily. These "looked like tiny grains of rice on the seams of garments."[127] Scratching bites brought about skin infections exacerbated by the unhygienic conditions of trench life. So the thought which lay behind the impregnated shirt and ointment would be appreciated.

---

[126] DeGroot p206
[127] Winter D p97

The need to know more about what was happening at the front was evident in the response to the film the Battle of the Somme. In Anstruther as elsewhere there were queues to see it. The attraction was partly the timeliness of it - the two official cameramen Geoffrey Malins and JB McDowell were in position to film the opening day of the battle and the film was first shown on 21 August 1916 when the scale of the slaughter would have begun to be realised. Above all however it was compelling because of its realism. Attention focussed in particular on a 21 second sequence which showed men climbing out of the trench and going over the top - and depicts a British soldier falling back into the trench. This cameo portrayal of the horrors of war which attracted attendances of over 20 million nationwide in the first six weeks, is now thought to have been faked.[128] Whether the scene was staged or not it faithfully represented the reality and allowed families to get close to the experience of their sons and husbands.

The clamour about the film may well have attracted local people to a war relics exhibition which was held in the Town Hall in September 1916. Thomas McWhirr an enterprising Glasgow man had made four journeys to the Flanders battlefields and was able to put on display 530 separate articles including British, French and German weapons, passports, maps, medals, darts, shells and glass said to come from the windows at Rheims.[129] It clearly drew the crowds as the exhibition raised £50 10/. However the organisers had to appeal for the return of 120 yards of Union Jack bunting which went missing from the Town Hall.[130]

Perhaps this was an indication of the rise in juvenile crime which was agitating the town and which was attributed to the absence of so many fathers from home, as well as to the pernicious effect of cinema. A fulminating editorial in the *East of Fife Record* suggested that the authorities should use the fascination with cinema to good effect by filming the birching of young offenders and showing it "in the picture palaces which youngsters frequent."[131] (Complaints about juvenile delinquency were widespread and although the level of recorded crime fell during the war, offences committed by juveniles rose. As well as the absence of fathers fighting abroad other contributory factors were thought to be women becoming too involved in worthy causes and children

---

[128] Reeves p786
[129] EoFR 21 September 1916
[130] EoFR 8 February 1917
[131] EoFR 26 October 1916

earning more money than ever before because of the opportunities afforded by war work and occupying roles vacated by those a few years older than them who had gone to war.)[132]

1916 ended functionally. Christmas Day was not celebrated, with shops remaining open and no services in the local churches. If the mood was sober after two years and more of war then it was to darken still further.

---

[132] DeGroot p221

Chapter 6

1917 - No End in Sight

By the beginning of 1917 the Western Front, and indeed the war, was beginning to take on an air of permanence. The shutter of trench lines which had descended at the beginning of 1915 remained virtually unchanged two years later. A line of devastation, caused by bombardment, fighting, and mining, stretched 400 miles from the North Sea to the Swiss border. This had been consolidated by digging and reinforcement with communication systems put in place (although the German efforts were almost always more permanent in feature than the British). Two years of trench warfare and the failure at the Somme in particular had shown how much easier it was to defend positions than to assault them. It was difficult to see how victory could be achieved.

Locally, conviction had remained strong that the war would not only be won but was being won. In August 1915, on the first anniversary of the war, the local paper had confidently concluded " Today [Germany] is to all intents a beaten nation ... (but) that does not mean that the end of the war is in sight. Those who should know count upon at least another 15 months of war - but it does mean that the end, come when it may will see the Allies victorious."[133] This was before the British war losses on an industrial scale which occurred in 1916 but even a year later the effects of Loos and then the Somme had not yet undermined popular willingness to prosecute the war. In some respects the war had to go on to a successful conclusion to avenge those lost and to justify their sacrifice. Even after the Somme the *East of Fife Record* could offer the opinion, in the autumn of 1916, that " while everything is progressing favourably for the allies we have to think about the end of the war." However it warned there should be no peace until Germany realises "it will have to make good, ton for ton, ships her submarines have unlawfully destroyed."[134]

The German submarine attacks on merchant shipping were held, particularly in this maritime community, to be as unspeakable as the Zeppelin attacks. Their shocking effect on the sensibilities of what passed as fair in war have been colourfully described "as if a respectable curate of your acquaintance were to whip out a revolver and demand your purse... the world did not anticipate the new code of morals, more

---

[133] EoFR 5 August 1915
[134] EoFR 21 September 1916

especially from a people of culture. Deceived by the spectacles and the missionary manner Britain left her merchant ships unarmed."[135]

It was one thing to be defiant in the face of such offence - it is another to maintain that stance when the attacks not only continue but are prosecuted ever more successfully. In August 1916, when the local newspaper was making its demands for reparations for shipping losses, 23 British merchant vessels were sunk at a cost of eight lives; in August 1917 it was 91 vessels at a cost of 462 lives. In 1916 in total 396 British merchant vessels were lost; in the following year nearly 1,200 were sunk or captured.[136] Herein lay the dilemma for the new British Prime Minister Lloyd George. He was reluctant to accede to General Haig's request for another major offensive on the Western Front given that British war losses stood at over 250,000 dead with little to show for it. The public might have turned against him if there were catastrophic losses with no military breakthrough. Yet simply to keep the war going was no easy option. Shipping losses were on such a scale that new building could replace only one ton in ten. Neutral ships were refusing to carry cargo to British ports. The British reserve of wheat dwindled to six weeks supply.[137] The question was, as Admiral Lord Fisher somewhat harshly put it, " Can the Army win the war before the Navy loses it".[138]

Whether or not the Navy was losing the war, it was certainly losing boats as it tried to combat the submarine menace, and Cellardyke men were going down with them. Drifters were often used for anti submarine work laying out nets of galvanised steel supported by hollow glass floats. Each net was 300 feet long and 30 feet deep. As each drifter carried ten nets a barrier 1,000 yards long could be laid out.[139] It was dangerous work although losses came often not from the submarines themselves but mines. Of the 86 hired trawlers which were lost in 1917, 56 were sunk by mines.[140] In 1917 down went Seaman James Dick in *HM Trawler Evadne* sunk by a mine off Owers light vessel, the 21 year old's death adding to the grief of his parents in George Street who had already lost his brother Andrew. Euphemia Henderson grievously mourned the loss of her 34 year old husband Mitchell, 1st engineer on *HM Trawler*

---

[135] Dixon pp.59-60

[136] Figures compiled from British Vessels lost at sea 1914-18 Table A p162

[137] Taylor p84

[138] Vansittart p155

[139] Jones p.70

[140] Figures compiled from lists in British vessels Lost at Sea pp.21-23

Morococala sunk by a mine off Daunt Rock Light Vessel. Mines would also account for the boats which were intended to clear away their menace. Some 1,700 ships and 25,000 men were involved in minesweeping. This was constant work as swept channels would be seeded with fresh mines laid from submarines. The mines themselves could be free floating or anchored under the surface; designed to explode on first contact or with a delay mechanism intended to maximise damage as the mine rolled along the hull of the ship.

Alex Keay, killed when his boat hit a mine

Alex Keay (25), mate on *HM Trawler Repro* was lost when it struck one of its quarries off Tod Head; lost too was another 25 year old John Christie, 2nd engineer, when *HMPMS Queen of the North* hit a mine off Orfordness.

The biggest local tragedy caused by mines in 1917 came well away from he naval front line however. Fishing was still taking place and in August the motor yawl *Jane* left Anstruther to join the herring boats off Eyemouth. She was skippered by Andrew Henderson who lived at 38 West Forth Street. As his crew began to haul in their nets they could feel that they were fouled and Henderson relayed this information to the officer in charge of the patrol boat escorting them. He was within a boat length when the mine entangled in the nets exploded. In a letter to Mrs Henderson he wrote "When the smoke and spray cleared away nothing whatever was to be seen except broken pieces of wood, and there was no sign of the crew... Before leaving the place I read the funeral service. I feel nothing I can say can really comfort you but we all consider that in meeting his death while working to bring food into the country he has given his life for our cause just as much as any man who does in the trenches."[141]

He was right that there was no comfort he could bring to Mrs Henderson - not only did she lose her husband but also her two sons Andrew of 28 James Street and Alexander who lived at 17 Rodger Street. Two other local men went down with them; 55 year old Thomas Boyter of 1 Rodger Street and James Wilson 6 Burnside Terrace. They were one crew amongst the 89 Scottish boats which were sunk while fishing.[142]

The war had come home to Cellardyke. Their deaths seemed to bring to a crescendo the feeling that the war had moved beyond a series of personal tragedies set against a backdrop of changed circumstances and impositions. It now was felt across the community and was ever present in terms of daily life.

Deaths such as these, as with the men at the front, were mourned at home in curtain-closed, gloom-filled houses with a monumental letter on the mantle piece. But the grief was personal to the families; there was little opportunity for the community to acknowledge the sacrifice - and clearly there was a craving to do so. In March 1917, sadly, such an opportunity arose.

David Clements, had been a student at agricultural college at the outbreak of the war. He had promptly joined up with the Fife and Forfar Yeomanry. Like other eager young men before him he was impatient at the delay in deploying to the front and so secured a transfer to the Royal Engineers. Sure enough he got to the front but was badly gassed in November 1916 and was invalided home. A week before his death he visited his family in Easter Pitkerie Farm "apparently feeling quite recovered and very fit." However on that visit he had a relapse and died. Conjecture was that "probably the rigours of 18 months soldiering and the effects of the gassing had more detrimentally affected his health than supposed." Although a sergeant he was still only 20. As his funeral cortege passed

---

[141] EoFR 16 August 1917

[142] Lee p89

Waid Academy it was flanked on both sides by the pupils, staff and rector of the school and a similar tribute was paid to the former pupil of Anstruther Easter School. (His father, also David, had been one of those who stood for election for the school board in 1914.)

His funeral took place around the same time as that of Captain John Thomson (47) the master of a Government requisitioned liner who had drowned in an accident off Portland, Dorset. These local funerals allowed the townsfolk to honour their dead not at a distance but in their midst. They acted, one suspects, as a proxy for all those whose bodies would never be lain to rest or who were buried beyond the capacity of parents to stand by their graveside. They were not recovered from the field of battle but in the opinion of the local paper "although neither of them were permitted to make the supreme sacrifice in the manner which we know they would have chosen, the readiness as Shakespeare says is all, and they will be numbered among our brave and honoured dead."[143]

The brave and honoured dead were to drastically accumulate over the coming weeks in a way which struck to the heart of Anstruther and Cellardyke. Lloyd George had decided to back a French plan for a two pronged attack which Somme-like would be preceded by a massive barrage. The French commander Nivelle (who was surprisingly afforded the role of supreme commander of allied forces by the British Prime Minister) was an artillery officer who still believed that a fearsome onslaught could provide the basis for a bursting through the German lines. The barrage, although more truncated than that which ushered in the Somme attack was nevertheless double in weight while it lasted. Although by this time some howitzers capable of high trajectory fire were in service on the Allied side and the guns were firing high explosive, nevertheless they were still predominantly old low trajectory, short distance weapons. The result, it has been said, was that the barrage churned up the ground over which the troops had to attack and the Germans were still in place able to line up their machine guns on the holes in the wire through which the attacking troops would have to funnel.

The British would attack at Arras a week earlier than the main French assault.

At the same time the Canadians were given Vimy Ridge to take. (Anstruther men continued to die in the Dominion's ranks. Pioneer James

---

[143] EoFR 22 March 1917

Anderson of the 54th Canadians was killed less than six weeks after arriving at the Western Front. A mason to trade he had emigrated six years previously to Vancouver.) The first day of the attack has been described as a success - trudging through the April sleet and rain behind a creeping barrage, inroads of up to three miles were made into the German positions. However on 10 April German reserves were moved up to plug the breach. Those first two days swept away two local Gordon Highlanders. Private Andrew Halcrow (27) of 22 John Street, a cooper, and Private James Lindsay (27) of Hadfoot Wynd died at Arras. Back home local people began to realise that a big push was on, as the columns of the paper filled with men killed. On April 17 the dead came from Anstruther, Cellardyke, Crail, Pittenweem, Colinsburgh, Elie and Arncroach. By that time an intermission had been called to allow the exhausted front-line troops to recover and to draft in replacements for the 20,000 casualties which the British side had suffered. However battle was set to resume on the 23rd April, and the same troops who led the charge on 9th April were expected to lead the new assault. This time of course the Germans were alert and well dug in. The 7th battalion Black Watch had been give only three days out of the front line when it was brought back in preparation for the resumption of the Battle of Arras. There was to be no repeat of the earlier success (when the Black Watch had lost 20 men in three days). At 4.45 am Captain the Reverend John Cargill led his men over the top. He had been the assistant minister at Scoonie Parish Church and was an East Fife man having been a pupil at Waid Academy and then graduated from St Andrews University. He had only joined up on 1 April 1916 as a private yet within a year he had been commissioned and promoted to Captain. Despite pushing his men on to attack hard on the heels of the British barrage the Scots found that the German machine guns were already pouring fire onto them. Bloodily they struggled up to the German defensive position only to find the wire uncut. The Black Watch were forced to fall into shell holes and for over four hours they lay there amongst dead and wounded comrades. Then lumbering across No Man's Land came a tank which was supposed to have been in support at the start of the attack. According to a Black Watch historian "As soon as the tank crossed the German wire and trench the enemy in the front line put up their hands."

(This account too readily maintains the impression that tanks had a decisive impact when they were deployed and struck immediate terror into defenders. More modern accounts are dismissive of the early tanks arguing that the technology was not well enough developed to provide an engine powerful enough to drive the speed of a 30 ton vehicle above 6 kilometres an hour. The US writer Mosier concludes "An object the size of a garage moving at the speed of a leisurely walk is an easy target to hit. Once German soldiers got over their immediate panic at this new weapon, they discovered it was easy to destroy." Vulnerability was compounded by unreliability with tanks constantly breaking down so that even by the time of Arras more than a half of tanks would be out of action within 24 hours of being deployed.[144])

However when a tank did get through it clearly did have an impact as on this occasion. German defenders were captured by the 7th who had followed up the tank "and many more were killed."[145] By the evening the Black Watch held the German trenches but the cost had been great. On that day the 7th Battalion lost seven officers killed and five wounded. Captain John Cargill died of his wounds on the following day.

It was becoming increasingly difficult for the British to maintain the Arras offensive. Losses were mounting and the reinforcements which were being pushed up to the line were not always up to to the job. Serious discontent broke out in the 8th Battalion Black Watch which had lost heavily in the initial assault. Nearly one hundred men were drafted in to bolster their numbers - but these were Army Service Corps men who had recently been in hospital. It must have been a moment of mutual shock when the two ranks realised what they were in for. Whether regarded as battle hardened or battle fatigued the fighting troops were now expected to accommodate men who were normally employed in driving trucks or supervising stores, some of whom were hardly able to load their rifles· Yet soldiers on the fighting line were paid much less than their Army Service Corps counterparts (who could receive up to six times the pay of an ordinary infantryman). The Commanding Officer fruitlessly protested and was given only two days to train the new draft in preparation for an attack on Greenland Hill on 3 May 1917. The results were predictable. Even with the reinforcements the 8th Battalion could only muster 10 officers and 470 other ranks (the nominal strength of a battalion was 1,000). For those like Signaller Hugh Dickson who had already fought to survive the first attack there must have been a feeling of imminent disaster as they waited for the signal to attack. The 24 year old from High Street Anstruther Wester had trained as a joiner but he had been employed on a drifter at the outbreak of the war. Being at sea must have seemed a better prospect than looking along the trenches at the understrength ranks, of which a quarter were inexperienced and

---

[144] Mosier pp.238-9
[145] Wauchope Vol. 2 pp284-5

untrained.

Disaster it proved to be. For some reason the zero hour was altered to 3.45 am. Into the dark they stumbled finding it impossible to keep in line because of the condition of the ground, barely knowing which way they were facing and only to find that the pre-dawn attack had not caught the Germans by surprise. The enemy were ready and waiting and opened up their machine guns into the gloom of No Man's Land. Within 15 minutes nearly half the battalion were killed or wounded. Of course Hugh Dickson was one of them.

Signaller Hugh Dickson, Killed in Battle of Arras

When the Arras offensive was finally called off in late June British losses were 120,000. Militarily, Arras reinforced the perception of the conflict's crushing permanence.

At home too the war took on a more institutionalised presence. Fund-raising events at the pictures had stopped with the introduction of the Amusement Tax which if it was applied elsewhere as it was in Anstruther seemed curiously regressive. On May 18th 1916 the revised prices to watch the double bill of 'The Evil Men Do' and 'Those Bitter Sweets' were given as Body of Hall 3d (previously 2d) and main gallery 8d (previously 6d).

However for those rich enough to be able to afford the 1 shilling to take a seat in the front gallery there was no increase on the previous charge. Under Lloyd George new ministries were developed - shipping, labour, food and national service - ushering in what has been described as a system of war socialism. These were intended to direct matters for the period of the conflict only, to be dismantled at the return of normality.

British merchant ships were requisitioned. Prices were controlled. In the case of bread, as the costs of imported wheat rose, this was done by means of Government subsidy. A war on waste was waged. A notice in the local press announced that waste food would be collected daily,[146] whilst waste paper was collected every Monday. To prevent waste being generated the government prohibited the printing of traders' circulars and posters

(When Anstruther Wester Town Council debated a request from the Local Government Board to co-operate with the waste collection scheme the idiosyncratic Provost Porter growled that their community had nothing to waste - they had no rich people making fortunes. This could be taken as a dig both at the profiteering of business men and the higher wages commanded by those working in the munitions industry.)

Government notices were now appearing in the local press on a regular basis. Anstruther's Post office was closed, with the officious announcement that this was "in consonance with the policy of retrenchment which is being pursued in all government departments at the present time."[147]

Throughout the late summer and autumn of 1917 desultory news came of other local men who would not come back - Robert Smith had arrived in the town in February 1914 to teach at Waid Academy and found himself interim headmaster until 1915 when he joined up with the Royal Scots. Lieutenant Smith was 29 when he fell whilst with the Machine Gun Corps.

Private George Corstorphine made it back to Blighty but died in Orpington hospital of shrapnel wounds to the neck. The 25 year old had joined up with the Black Watch at the start of the war and had already survived being wounded at the battle of Loos. He was brought home to be buried at Kilrenny Kirkyard.

---

[146] CBO 17 April 1917

[147] CBO 17 April 1917

Surviving a battle is no guarantee of surviving the war of course and some soldiers seemed destined not to make it. Take Alexander Boyter. The 24 year old former spinner at the local rope works had joined up at the start with the Black Watch Territorials. His was a catalogue of mishap, of being in the wrong place at the wrong time. He was seriously wounded in the eye early in the war and after recovering at home (where he used his time encouraging others to join up) was back at the front when he was badly burnt. He then subsequently escaped death when a section of sandbags collapsed killing one of his party and breaking the back of another. Private Boyter however survived the Third Battle of Ypres and after a period in training camp returned to the front line with the 6th Battalion Black Watch. The regimental account laconically notes that particular tour of duty passed with little worthy of record except that on the 16 September the enemy attacked three posts of which two had to be evacuated. In the grand scheme of things this was of course unremarkable but it was those attacks which finally put paid to Alex Boyter who had suffered so much for King and country. His company captain wrote to his parents at 5 George Street that their son had been inside a concrete building when an enemy shell exploded outside and a fragment flew through the window hitting him in the head and, they were assured, killing him instantaneously. There was nothing heroic about being unlucky, as poor Alex seems to have been for all his war yet Captain Brown wanted to give his parents the knowledge that their son, whose passing would not even merit a mention in regimental notes after the war, was a man of worth, telling them, "It is a great blow to me to lose one of my best stretcher bearers for I always look upon them as the bravest and best of men."[148]

Alex Boyter had been one of the local men who had received the gift of cigarettes from a benefit event. Shortly before his death he had written a poignant note to Mrs Georgina Murray the organiser to thank her and to say that he had seen her husband Col. Murray once but did not have a chance of speaking to him. He assured her that he was getting along fine although briefly acknowledging his most recent brush with death saying that he had "a narrow escape last time" before concluding " I hope that Anstruther is always lively and having plenty visitors. I think the town has done its duty in this terrible struggle for liberty."[149]

It was a view shared by most and some were beginning to question whether the struggle was worth the sacrifice. By the early autumn of 1917 the editorial in the local press gave voice to what was clearly being

---

[148] CBO 17 September 1917
[149] CBO 23 August 1917

widely felt throughout the country and not just in east Fife. "The unspoken thought is that if we do not break down their resistance next year we shall have to give up." It was scathing of "loud professions of our being able and willing to go on for as many years as may be needed. That sort of thing goes down with nobody nowadays."

The failure to make ground in the Arras and Ypres offensives was depressing - so many men lost and still so little to show for it. Still the newspaper hung onto the hope that attrition would cause German resolve to collapse. But "if we had to get to the Rhine at the rate of say a mile per month we might as well stop the war now."[150]

Despondency was justified. Yet despite the costly failure of Arras to provide the kind of breakthrough which would represent the breaking of a dam, flooding troops behind German defences and precipitating a collapse, the Allied commanders opened up a new offensive at Ypres.

The approach to the battle was familiar but magnified. The pre-attack bombardments were becoming ever more ferocious. The Somme was preceded by a bombardment which was the greatest in military history and expected to remove all vestige of German resistance. The third Battle of Ypres surpassed the Somme by an astonishing fourfold - 4 million shells crashed on German lines.

In the British trenches the packed masses of attacking troops would have to hope that the weight of the assault, as well as the presence of 136 tanks, would make the difference this time.

The preparations for the attack had been thorough. The 9th Battalion Black Watch which had a rough time just getting to the front had been employed in bringing in the Belgian harvest. The fields were needed for training and once cleared were staked out with flags to represent the German trench systems which were to be the objective.

At 3.50 am on 31st July the practice was over - it was for real. The Black Watch with tanks in support attacked over the uneven, cratered and shell-pocked surface. The assault smashed its way through the German front lines, and battled up to the second line of trenches 500 yards back despite heavy fire from snipers and machine guns. The curtain of artillery fire had done its job and had cut the enemy wire so that the Black Watch could maintain the momentum of its assault. The Scottish soldiers drove

---

[150] CBO 13 September 1917

1,500 yards behind the front line before their charge faltered as the German counter attack from field guns was too much to bear. The battalion had suffered 226 casualties on that first day assault on Pilckem Ridge. It took the life of Lance Corporal Brodie. We know nothing of how he died except that he was killed in action. We do know that he did not want to be there. His father, Baillie Brodie, had argued strenuously at the local tribunal that his 27 year old son should be exempted from call up - his cleekmaking business could not afford to lose skilled men like his sons. Now he was lost for good.

This was Passchendaele in which the conditions for war were impossible - untold numbers of wounded men died in flooded shell holes as the rain poured down. In all 70,000 soldiers were killed and 170,000 wounded with nothing to show for it, and even worse perhaps little to justify it.

But while it might be acceptable to wonder at the course of the war it was not deemed permissible to question the cause for the conflict. Few seemed to doubt that the Germans were the aggressors, that their militarism had caused them to seek to take advantage of circumstances, to flout norms and to provoke Britain to come to the defence of otherwise defenceless neighbours.

Apoplexy was induced locally, therefore, at a sermon which had been preached by the United Free Church in Colinsburgh. The Reverend Revie had denounced militarism, implicating Britain. This was too much for the editor of the *Coast Burgh Observer* whose language was roseately ringing: "we believe that the war was forced upon us, that we and our allies are fighting a great cause, a holy cause according to the church. Has Scottish blood flowed like water, have we given our sons, our fathers, our all to be denounced by a Minister of the United Free Church ?" This was rhetorical question of course, but for good measure the paper supplied its own thunderous response "No - a thousand times no. To the dead who died for the liberty that is ours; to the glorious heroes of 1914 onwards and to the yet unborn we should be traitors... if we acquiesced in his remarks."[151]

The scale of the sacrifice was such that it was unconscionable to fail to distinguish between the aggressors and those forced to respond. For many, whatever the advisability of going to war, the manner in which Germany had prosecuted the war was sufficient reason for war to be waged. An indignant letter writer, responding to the Reverend Revie's

---

[151] CBO 8 November 1917

sermon, summed up the catalogue of grievances which required redress "has he never heard of the unspeakable tortures inflicted upon the Belgians, French, Polish, Serbians and Roumanians... the martyrdom of Nurse Cavell and Captain Fryatt... the unutterable horrors of the German prison camps. The sinking of the Lusitania and the more recent air raids on London."[152]

The elevation of the war to a latter-day holy crusade was not shared by all of those who had much to lose. 'A Mother' wrote expressing the dread and bitterness which was being experienced by those who were being compelled to fight: "I have two sons in the trenches who never to my knowledge expressed the least desire to go and fight for a just cause as it is termed and perhaps die a glorious death. I for one should not envy the tribunal members who have forced our young lads to go out and get butchered. Look at the suffering the war is causing - picture the agonies of parents who have sons in the fighting line dreading the hour when bad news may come of their loved ones... and all this is the outcome of the militarism which has taken hold of our country - a militarism which responsible people tell us we are fighting to subdue."[153]

Mothers will mourn - that is one certainty of war. For some there was no mothers to mourn them but they would be embraced in the thoughts of others. James Hepburn had been a well known face in Anstruther . He had been born in the town and went to Waid Academy. His family home was in the High Street and he could be found at work just a few minutes walk from there in the Post Office which he joined after leaving school. But as the local paper approvingly noted he was an aspiring young man and set off to London to further his career with the Thames Coal Company. He joined up with the 1st London Postal Rifles, rather than return home to join a Scottish battalion but he did come back to Anstruther to see his widowed mother in August 1917. However she was frail and died only three weeks after his visit. In November 28 year old Private Hepburn was in the trenches when an attack took place. According to the Rifles chaplain a German bomb was thrown killing Hepburn as well as "his great friend Captain Douglas."[154] It is clear that this friendship was well established and well known. Indeed the mother of Captain Douglas wrote to say that at her son's memorial service in Kent she had included Hepburn's name "knowing of their warm friendship for each other."[155]

---

[152] CBO 15 November 1917

[153] CBO 15 November 1917

[154] Captain A.G. Douglas, London Regiment (London Scottish) 14th Battalion. Died 30 November 1917.

[155] CBO 27 November 1917

Friendship between officers and men is held to be uncommon. According to DeGroot, so far as most middle class officers were concerned "ordinary soldiers were not only a different class they were virtually a different species."[156] Officers even though they shared the trenches lived different lives from their men - they slept apart, ate apart, went to their own cinemas and brothels. It is possible of course that Captain Douglas was only a temporary gentleman promoted because of the exigencies of war rather than background and natural rank. In the war 43% of commissions were granted to NCOs compared with 2% prior to the war; and around 40% of temporary officers were from working class or lower middle class backgrounds.[157] It is said that army elites despaired at the new breed of officers who were too familiar with their men. (Or any familiarity which threatened the established hierarchy, however petty. Robert Graves in 'Good-bye to All That' recalls his commanding officer ordering field punishment for a private who dared to call a Lance Corporal by his first name - and court martialled the NCO for permitting it.)

Promotion from the ranks was the normal route for Anstruther men to be commissioned. There are 10 army officers on the two memorials.[158] Some were ex army regulars who returned to the colours. Others were professional or landed gentlemen. They were teachers, clergymen, university students. These were local golden boys - not an elite but achievers who were a source of pride. Lieutenant Philip Oliphant Ray was perhaps the nearest Anstruther had to a young romantic dashing officer. He was well known, the second son of the Rev. James Ray the popular minster at Cellardyke who by 1917 had gone to take up a new congregation in Portobello. The family were clearly proud of their son - his progress in Glasgow University exams towards his engineering degree was reported in the press. But Philip did not finish his course. His father had said that young men of Anstruther would rise willingly and promptly when danger threatened Britain. His middle son was one of the first to do so. (After academic research abroad the oldest son, Robert, BSc, FRS, FRSSA offered his services to the government as a scientist and in 1916 became Chemist in Charge of the Nitro Glycerine Section of HM Factory Gretna.[159])

Unlike others of his background Philip Ray did not seek a commission, even though he had been a member of the Officer Training Corps at

---

[156] DeGroot p167

[157] Ferguson p348

[158] Excluding Captain Black, who held his commission from the Territorials but was at 55 never on active service.

[159] EoFR 26 February 1916

University. Instead he joined the Cameronians as a private, going to the front in July 1915. He seems to have always been on the look out for action - by the Battle of Loos he was a lance corporal in charge of a machine gun unit. He wrote a long account home of how his unit moved up to the front line arriving there just before midnight: "Rain still fell but most of us had a good sleep for an hour or two in the trenches with nothing else for shelter than a waterproof sheet. The artillery roared all night. When clear enough the gas and smoke could be seen being slowly wafted to the German lines. Shortly afterwards a shout went up, the attack had commenced." After the battle where he had seen many casualties he expressed his wonderment that he had survived: "How I ever came out of it I do not know; my gun was hit once by a bullet and twice with shrapnel while I was carrying it."[160]

He was offered a commission and was made a second lieutenant in the 8th Battalion Black Watch. By October 1916 he can be found having to write letters of condolence home to the families of local men who were his contemporaries. Maybe it was his engineering background which drew him to aviation, maybe it was the opportunity to rise above trench warfare. Whatever the reason, by the time Arras came around he was attached to the 59th Squadron, Royal Flying Corps based at Bellevue about 20 miles north east of Amiens. This squadron was new to the front having arrived only in February 1917. It was equipped with 21 R.E.8s a new type of two seater plane which rapidly acquired an evil reputation. When it first arrived at the front it had a marked tendency to spin, leading to fatal flying accidents. And if it did crash and pitch on its nose it would almost certainly burst into flames as the engine was pushed back into the emergency and main fuel tanks - leading to the immolation of crews who survived crash landings.

By 1917 the Royal Flying Corps had developed its functions so that it had fighters to aggressively patrol over enemy lines; bombers to attack strategic targets; spotter planes to assist the artillery in finding its range on a target and reconnaissance planes which flew photograph missions to capture images of troop and artillery movements. However although the British had more machines the Germans were technically superior in planes and pilots. In a dogfight the British planes were outperformed and losses were high and inevitably the replacement pilots were less experienced and skilled than their German opponents. German aces became household names. By 1917 the legendary aces such as Immelman and Boelcke had been succeeded by the even more feted Baron von

---

[160] EoFR 14 October 1915

Richthofen. At the beginning of 1917 von Richthofen was given command of his own Jagdstaffel, and was awarded the Orden Pour le Merite, the coveted Blue Max. (He was not quite yet the Red Baron as he had only recently painted his Albatross in the famous all red livery.)

In the gunsights of such experienced fighter pilots, reconnaissance planes in particular were sitting ducks. Yet their work was vital in terms of establishing enemy positions, gauging the success of bombardments and, once a battle was underway, reporting whether infantry had actually broken through to their objectives. To protect them, fighter aircraft were required to fly escort. Usually the fighters did not take off with the two seaters but were expected to meet up with them in the air. However in an age when there was no air to air, or even ground to air, radio communication this could be a hit or miss affair.

When the battle of Arras begun the RFC were expected to be busy in support. But on April 9 1917, Easter Monday there was a drizzle of snow and visibility was poor. The aerial bombing programme was cancelled and offensive patrols curtailed. So when the first day of fine weather broke every plane took to the air.

At 8.15 am on 13 April six R.E.8s of 59 Squadron set off once more to photograph the Drocourt-Queant line. Philip Ray was the one given the responsibility of getting the pictures[161] in a plane flown by another Scotsman, Lieutenant Philip Bentinck Boyd of the Gordon Highlanders.[162] The others were there to provide close escort, as the R.E.8s did have the capacity to defend itself if it could get the forward firing Vickers synchronised gun lined up or the observer could swing his Lewis gun on the enemy. But in reality they needed more cover than that. For the reconnaissance to be successful they needed to fly attentively along the whole line of their objective, and that would take them close to Douai aerodrome where von Richthofen was based. It was intended then that the R.E.8s would meet up with the offensive fighter patrols in the area - Spads, F.E.2ds and Bristol Fighters. Needless to say this did not happen. The Spads were 20 minutes late in taking off; the F.E.2ds got caught up in a dogfight and the Bristol Fighters saw nothing of the reconnaissance planes. So on flew the 59th squadron's isolated planes. And down onto

---

[161] Franks et al p109. According to H.A. Jones (p350) two of the aircraft carried cameras, but Franks et al claim that only Ray's plane A3203 was equipped for photography.

[162] Son of Mr and Mrs John Gamble Boyd, 35 Elgin Avenue, Toronto; husband of Drouth Richardson (formerly Boyd.)

them plunged six German single seaters led by von Richthofen himself. (This was not his famous circus, which actually appeared for the first time on the following day.) There was no contest - the evidence appears to show the R.E.8s desperately trying to get away and being rapaciously hunted down by the Germans. All six planes were shot down.[163] Von Richthofen scored the 41st kill of his career in the attack. Philip Ray was killed not by the Red Baron but fell perhaps to his brother Lothar von Richthofen who got two British planes. On that day, 13 April 1917 he was posted missing, presumed dead. In one of those sad coincidences of history, it was his father's birthday. Reverend Ray, unaware of his son's loss, quietly turned 58. Philip would remain forever just 23 years old.

---

[163] Jones pp.350-351

Chapter 7

1918 - The Turning Tide

The casualties of assaults along the Western front were not just the dead and wounded but also the missing. Relatives would be left with no news. Was their son dead, lost on the battlefield? Was he in hospital but unable to get word home? Or had he been taken prisoner? By 1918 the local paper was beginning to fill up with reports filtering back from men who were prisoners of war.

Of course men had been captured throughout the war. The first account of a local prisoner of war came as early as 29 October 1914 when Thomas McCutcheon, the 3rd engineer on the Clan liner *Benmohr,* was reported to be in Germany. His ship had been rammed by the German cruiser *Emden* and subsequently scuttled with no loss of lives. Given that this incident took place on 16 October it seems remarkable that news of his whereabouts was in a local weekly less than a fortnight later.

More usually families could have a long anxious wait. James Smith a sailmaker in School Wynd had a miserable Christmas in 1916 wondering about the fate of his 39 year old son William, a private in the Highland Light Infantry, who had been posted missing from 18 November.[164] A postcard was eventually received in February of the following year from the ex-Windygates miner saying he was a POW in Germany [165]

News of the fate of such men did not always come through promptly or even from official sources. Many local men had gone off in their drifters; some of them were as far away as the Adriatic attempting to stop Austrian submarines from passing through the straits of Otranto. They had laid out anti submarine nets across the gulf and 100 drifters patrolled its length, dropping explosive charges when they suspected a submarine had broken through. On 17 May 1917 the Austrians decided to clear away this obstacle and sent destroyers supported by submarines and spotter planes in what was one of the first three-dimensional attacks of the war, engaging assets in the air, on the sea and under the waves. The lightly armed converted fishing boats were no match for the naval vessels, although doggedly one skipper refused to surrender and fought back with his puny 57mm gun, saving his boat and gaining himself the Victoria Cross. Most others had no chance to escape and in what became known

---

[164] EoFR 28 December 1916
[165] CBO 15 February 1917

as the Battle of Otranto, 14 drifters were sunk, including the *Craignoon* from Anstruther and the *Felicitas* from Buckhaven. Nearly 100 Allied sailors died, but the Austrians had allowed many more to surrender before sinking their boats.

Craignoon, local drifter sunk at the Battle of Otranto

News of the Austrian navy attacks on the Adriatic drifters had a terrible effect on the East Neuk as the Admiralty reported simply that the crews were missing believed lost. The initiative to find out what had actually befallen them was taken by Alex Watson the oilskin factory owner who also happened to be a major shareholder in the drifter *Craignoon*. He, along with the Anstruther fishery officer and the local GP, contacted the International Red Cross which, in turn, made representations to the Austrian Government. In this way they were able to establish that even though the *Craignoon* had been sunk the crew had been rescued and were prisoners of war.[166]

In July 1917 George Watson from Burnside was also known to be a prisoner in Austria after surviving the sinking of the *Felicitas*.[167] He sent a postcard through the Red Cross to his uncle George Doig of West

---

[166] Watson, p187
[167] CBO 12 July 1917

Forth Street, letting him know that he was alright but that yet another prisoner in his POW camp had died. George was the young Cellardyke sailor who had joined up to get a smart uniform to impress the girls. That must have seemed an age ago. The effect of long war and an uncertain future deep inside enemy country clearly had its impact. "I wish I saw the war over" he wrote, adding "I am getting fed up with this prisoner's life now."

Prisoner of war card sent by young seaman George Watson

Clearly there were cases of previous captures which had gone unreported. For instance in January 1918 James Wilson of 9 Rodger Street Cellardyke was awarded the Serbian Gold medal for services in British drifters in the Adriatic in the winter of 1915-16, it being mentioned incidentally that he was currently a POW.

Towards the end of the war the detailing of the whereabouts of POWs substantially increased. POWs such as James Trainer were regularly in the news in 1918. He had been a slater with Gilmour in West Anstruther and was captured in France whilst serving with the Royal Naval Division (having previously survived the action at Suvla Bay where he had been wounded in the eye).

But for families news of their son being a prisoner of war was mixed. Of course there would be the relief that he was alive. But German treatment of prisoners of war was felt to be harsh (and as we have seen was cited as one of the reasons why war must waged to a successful conclusion). Local first hand accounts gave credence to tales of cruel behaviour. In January 1918 Private William Smith managed to get a postcard home to say that he had been released from Ruhleben and was on his way to Switzerland. He said he had been reduced to a skeleton by starvation after being captured in November 1916. Once in hospital in the Mont Blanc hotel he detailed how four of his comrades were shot for taking a piece of bread from a French civilian, with the rest of them forced to watch the execution which presumably served as *une example pour les autres*. Forced labour for prisoners could be expected and Smith spent six months digging trenches before collapsing of exhaustion which precipitated his transfer. He said the hard work and starvation rations caused 1,000 Russians to die from want.[168]

Others reported back cheerily however that conditions were not so bad. Private William Birrell, the son of Birrell the baker Anstruther, was in hospital after being wounded then captured in March 1918. He claimed that he was "now as well as ever he was in his life and in no hurry to quit the hospital where the bed is always at his disposal." He was busy being the head chef, cooking porridge for his colleagues with the oats which had arrived with some other hospital comforts.

Whilst it was good to hear that he was well, the paper could not help but note that "the vein of this communication is in striking contrast to that contained in some others that have been received from prisoners of war in Germany."[169]

William Birrell's letter showed the benefit of receiving parcels from home noting that the first they had received was from the Perthshire Prisoners of War Association which had been dispatched on June 20th and received just over a month later.

In Anstruther the formidable fund-raising efforts were swung behind providing comforts for POWs. A concert was held in June 1918 raising £53. The following month the £60 raised by the pupils of Cellardyke school was split between the ever-present need of the Sphagnum Moss Work Party and POW Funds. As usual the organisers wanted to ensure that it was local men who benefited so when the cash was sent to the

---

[168] EFO 24 January 1918
[169] EFO 12 September 1918

Fund HQ they took care to draw attention to the names of local lads who were POWs.[170] There were plenty of names to include; Private Donaldson of Cards Wynd who used to be in the North of Scotland Town and County Bank; Private William Leslie, printer; Private Robert Meldrum; Private Robert Wood who lived at 21 Rodger Street.

(Whilst the clothing, food and cigarettes in these parcels would be welcomed the brisk efforts of Mary Bethune, were rather less indulgent. She had set about soliciting books to be sent out to POWs but insisted that these had to be educational requesting contributions on history, geology, logic, mathematics, surgery etc. to be sent to her home in High Street Elie.)[171]

Surrendering to become a prisoner of war was no guarantee of safe passage. There has been heated debate as to the treatment meted out to those holding up their hands. Soldiers have claimed that prior to the battle of the Somme they were ordered to show no quarter to the enemy and that no prisoners were to be taken. It is said that this instruction was repeated in three different divisions massing for the attack but always verbally, never by written order.[172] The pressure came not just from the top but from the training ground - new arrivals to the infamous base at Etaples were warned by hard bitten instructors that "every prisoner means a day's rations gone."[173]

Certainly soldiers carried out what they believed to be more than virtual orders. A Private Arthur Hubbard of the London Scottish provided his own account "we had strict orders not to take any prisoners, no matter if wounded. My first job was, when I had finished cutting some of their wire away, to empty my magazine on three Germans that came out of their deep dugouts, bleeding badly and put them out of their misery. They cried for mercy, but I had my orders - they had no feelings whatever for us poor chaps."[174]

Even if a combatant did successfully manage to surrender without being mown down, there was no guarantee of safe passage into captivity. Robert Graves regarded the murder of prisoners as commonplace. "The commonest motives were, it seems, revenge for deaths of friends or

---

[170] EFO 20 June 1918
[171] EFO 11 April 1918
[172] Middlebrook p94
[173] Brown M p28
[174] Brown M p116-7

relatives, jealousy of the prisoner's trip to a comfortable prison camp in England, military enthusiasm, fear of being suddenly overpowered or more simply impatience with the escorting job."[175]

Others have protested strongly that the British soldier was by nature "a friendly man who treated his captives well once the heat of battle had passed"[176] and that the killing of prisoners was a rare phenomenon of the war even if it undoubtedly took place.

Whether rare or not Fife men were implicated. The *Coast Burgh Observer* had carried a first hand account from a local Royal Scot of his first experience of a raid on German trenches: "We carried out a successful raid against the Germans killing quite a number and taking a few prisoners. One of the Germans when being escorted back lay down and refused to budge. A sergeant major placed a bomb in his trouser leg and left him. A bomb takes five seconds to explode after the pin has been drawn, so that you have an idea where that German is now."[177]

The fact that this could be reported in what was a controlled press and the jocular nature of the reference seems to indicate that this type of behaviour was not seen as as an atrocity and was clearly not a unique way of disposing of prisoners. There are accounts elsewhere of hand grenades being put in prisoner pockets, a private in the Green Howards recalling that "when it went off we all laughed."

A partial justification of such action was that Germans could not be trusted even after they had surrendered. There were manifold accounts of Germans surrendering, only to open fire with concealed weapons when their captors had lowered theirs. Back in 1915 an Anstruther man, George McKane of the 4th Black Watch, was wounded when a German prisoner he was escorting back to the British lines shot him with a revolver.[178]

The news of the prisoners of war did not eclipse the fact that men were still being lost and were not going to come back. It appears that relatives were only too ready to fear the worst, causing the local paper to wonder if this fatalism was justified. "Anxiety is filling many hearts just now. Day after day letters are eagerly awaited for - often in vain. Day after

---

[175] Graves p191

[176] Middlebrook p184

[177] CBO 13 September 1917

[178] EoFR 7 October 1915

day the same question is asked, any news from the front and often the answer is the same. Suspense develops into despair and though no news official or unofficial has been received I have repeatedly heard people sadly speak of their hero sons as amongst the missing."[179]

The reason for this and indeed for the increase in the numbers of POWs was perhaps the developments in the war in the early part of 1918. The constrained dynamic of the prolonged struggle was about to be changed. The Americans had joined the war and pumping men and *materiel* into the stalemate of the Western front threatened to shift the balance overwhelmingly in the favour of the Allies. The Germans knew this. If they were to be victorious they had to achieve a breakthrough before the American forces were at the front in sufficient numbers. By the spring of 1918 they just happened to be in a position to contemplate a major offensive as the withdrawal of the Russians from the war after the Bolshevik revolution permitted the redeployment of troops from the eastern front to the western lines - giving Germany at one point a significantly superior advantage in numbers. However the cost of years of bloodletting had drained German manpower - any assault had to be successful as there were no reserves to call upon. The whole generation of fighting age men was either in uniform, dead or crippled. If it was now, it would be never again for the Germans.

On the British side the privations of war were also evidently being felt. In February 1918 the 4/5 Black Watch were in the line at Guidencourt. The soldiers were expected to be scavengers. Special orders had been issued as to salvage and every man on leaving the trench area was expected to bring back some salved article with him. A divisional order was published weekly giving the value of the articles salved by unit. There was no apparent lack of material as it was said that the whole front was littered with rifles, overcoats, tents, bicycles, ammunition, Lewis guns - the debris left behind by the British on their retirement.

During this scavenging spell at the front, which was officially regarded as quiet, the usual lottery of life and death had taken Private Alex Doig of 3 Castle Street Anstruther. Previously a coachman at Grangemuir he had joined up nine months previously. A brief war and brief mention in the paper and another name crossed out.

Except that his granddaughter who herself was born in the home at 3 Castle Street still lives only a few yards away from there. So we know

---

[179] EFO 25 April 1918

that Alex was born on 23 November 1880 at 11 Heriot Terrace, Canonmills,

Private Alex Doig with his family

Edinburgh. His father, James, was also a coachman. We know what he looks like as he had a portrait photo taken by CFS Burrows in Anstruther (Mr Burrows, who was also the projectionist at the weekly cinema, had a studio in town). Alex was 33 when he married Helen Young, a 28 year old Anstruther woman, in what was the Young family house in Castle Street (Alex as a coachman lived at South Lodge on the Grangemuir estate). In the last photo taken of him, ghostly faded, he is in his uniform standing next to his little two year old daughter Mary and his wife Helen who has baby Jim in her arms. He was killed soon after and we know exactly how he died. In a front line trench he took the chance to exchange a few words with his brother-in-law Lance Corporal Jock Young who was serving with 1/7 Black Watch. He was the last person he spoke to. Jock saw him killed by a shell burst. The little New Testament of S/21949 Pte A Doig 4/6 Black Watch BEF France was sent home, perforated by shrapnel.

By the following month the Germans were ready for their offensive. On 21 March the so-called Michael Offensive was launched in the area of the old Somme battlefield. The German tactics were to rush forward, following a surprise bombardment, seeking to punch holes deep into the British defences.

Traditionally commanders would worry about assault troops being exposed on the flanks of an attack and being cut off. Now the Germans used stormtrooper tactics which rapidly gained ground and forced the British to abandon artillery and to retreat in disarray. On the first day the British losses were 7,000 dead and 21,000 taken prisoner (compared to the 20,000 dead and wounded on the first day of the Somme but with very few prisoners.) It is quite likely therefore that the increase in the numbers of the POWs reported in Anstruther is linked to the success of the German offensive when, for the first time in trench war, Britain found itself overrun and losing significant ground and men. Certainly local people knew something big was going on as the pages filled up with lists of dead, wounded and missing. The list on April 4 included Private Swinton, wounded and gassed; Private George Nicol, gunshot wound in neck and left eye; Private James Woodward wounded in left arm; Private W Neilson, gunshot wound in thigh.

Men still found time to get messages home and news from the front, from local sources, was an important source of information. When Wilfrid Bonthron was captured this was seen by another local man, the son of Niven the gardener at Grangemuir, and was reported back to his family in early April 1918 even though official word only came to them in June.

Similarly Lance Corporal Henry Boyter's capture was witnessed by a fellow soldier even though he was officially reported missing.[180] (Subsequently a postcard dated 4 April was received confirming his POW status).[181]

From a letter from the front we have a first-hand account of the German push by an Anstruther man in the Argyll and Sutherland Highlanders 7th Battalion. Lance Corporal John Thomson wrote to his parents at 22 James Street in Cellardyke:

"Fritz started his push on Thursday and I was supposed to go on leave on Saturday so if the push had been a few days later I would have been home and reading about it in Blighty. We have been in the line for 25

---

[180] EFO 2 May 1918
[181] EFO 23 May 1918

days - 20 days before the push and five days in the thick of it. The first day of the attack Fritz attacked on our right and left, his intentions being I believe to try to cut off the division. In this he failed but not completely - the Black Watch were almost surrounded and have suffered greatly. Then followed the rearguard actions, four times did we extricate ourselves from the serious situation.

Machine guns were firing in front, on right and left sometimes in our rear. The Germans were in countless numbers so that we had no chance, but they did not attack in our immediate front - they simply came in hordes attempting to come round in our rear. They nearly succeeded on a few occasions. We just retired in time but not without causing him a lot of casualties. It seemed the more we shot the more seemed to take their place. I could go a parcel and some socks now as Fritz has captured our all."

(He never got his socks. Within days of getting this letter from their 20 year old son his parents were told that he had been admitted to hospital with shrapnel wounds to his thigh and died on 9 June.)

The blanks in his censored letter possibly referred to the 9th and 6th battalions of the Black Watch.

The 9th Battalion Black Watch found themselves forced to retreat three times within a morning as a German offensive outside of Arras overwhelmed their front line, bombed its way along the trench and broke through hastily erected defensive positions. Private William Dickson of A company was one of 250 battalion casualties. His parents in High Street Anstruther Wester were told that he had been wounded but clung to the hope that he had been taken prisoner. He was only 19 and was the brother of Signaller Hugh Dickson who had died less than a year before.

The 6th Battalion fared even worse. The March offensive had plunged them into five days of continuous fierce fighting which had shattered the ranks with 20 officers and 620 men being lost. The battalion effectively required to be rebuilt. The remnants mustered at a place called Burbure and large numbers of officers and soldiers, many of them very young, were drafted in. Specialist training was needed before the battalion could ever be an effective fighting force - Lewis gunners had to be formed into teams; stretcher bearers and signallers had to be found and trained. Yet there was no time.

On 9 April the German commander Ludendorff launched his second offensive, this time code-named "George". The strength of the attack, which aimed to capture the channel coast behind Ypres, was so powerful that it threatened to repeat the breakthrough achieved by the Germans in the March offensive. General Haig was forced to issue an order for last ditch resistance: "With our backs to the wall and believing in the the justice of our cause each one of us must fight on to the end... every position must be held on to the last man."[182]

And to the last boy. The young soldiers of the 6th Battalion were brought out of reserve to plug the gap . On the west bank of the Lawe river they fought to stem the German assault. Another 19 year old lad went missing, later to be presumed dead. Private Andrew Dick, whose parents lived at 14 East Forth Street Cellardyke was also a second son to be lost. But although youthful he does not appear to have been one of the recent and untried reinforcements which shored up the 6th battalion. Quite the opposite - he is said to have joined up at the start of the war and had been on active service for three years. In that time he had been twice wounded and gassed once. He had been hurt to such an extent that he was brought home and convalesced in Elie hospital. He had only returned to the front six weeks previously. This would mean that this veteran had joined up at 15 and was in the frontline as a 16 year old.

He was far from alone in doing so of course. At the outset of the war soldiers were supposed to be 19 before they could serve abroad. Given that the Territorial accepted boys of 17 into their ranks, many of them simply shipped off with their older mates. Some Regular soldiers were already veterans at an early age. A local boy Private Thomas Martin was wounded when fighting with the 2nd Black Watch in Tigris and was in hospital in Bombay in March 1916, the local paper noting with no particular surprise that he had celebrated his 17th birthday in the trenches of France.

Those joining up in 1914 had to be 5'3' tall, and have a minimum chest measurement of 34 inches. Thousands of boys managed to pass themselves off as 19, often lying about their exact age, sometimes it is said with the encouragement of Recruiting Sergeants who got two shillings and sixpence for each man attested into the infantry. Many parents were aghast to find out what had happened without their permission and pressure grew throughout the war to have under-age soldiers brought home or at least taken out of the front line, although the Government

---

[182] Keegan p434

persisted in the view that no boys had been enlisted with the knowledge of the War Office and "if boys under the proper age have been enlisted, it is their fault for having made a false declaration."[183] Others however seemed to be there with the full knowledge of their parents.

Once parents had let their sons go they could spend weeks and months wracked with worry. Lieutenant Thomas Smith's frontline service lasted no more than two months in total, yet it was a constant cause of dread and anguish to his parents who lived at 6 Rodger Street Cellardyke.

Lieutenant Thomas Smith-
former Dux of Waid Academy

They had received a telegram only a month after he had left for the front saying that he was missing. Fearing the worst they then received another saying he was accounted for in hospital in Rouen where he had been taken after being wounded by shrapnel in the chest. His wounds were such that by October 1916 he was in hospital in Aberdeen. It was not until April 1918 that he was deemed fit enough to return to active service. On May 16 he led a raid on German lines in which Smith's force killed several Germans and took seven prisoners. Having ordered his men to

---

[183] van Emden p.169

withdraw, the last that was seen of the young Royal Scots officer was as he sought to ensure that a wounded private also made it back. Smith's commanding officer wrote to his parents offering them some hope that their son had been taken prisoner as the Germans had reported having captured an officer and a private soldier from the Royal Scots. In fact this proved to be the case - but it did not secure his survival as the Red Cross in Geneva reported in October 1918 that Thomas Smith had died - aged only 21. He was one of the boys in the school hockey team captured in the photograph printed in the local paper in 1914. The paper had also recorded his exam passes which had equipped him to enter St Andrews University, where in March 1916 he passed in Greek, Latin and Mathematics. His parents were obviously so proud of him - they had presented him with a gold watch engraved 'Dux of Waid Academy 1914-1915.' For his fisherman father William, skipper of the *Olive Leaf*, and his mother Maggie the loss of their first born was grievous.

The time-lapsed flow of dispassionate information from the front which by turns elevated or crushed parental hopes could be cruel. Up at Mount Stuart, outside Elie, James and Ann Lindsay Cairns were equally shattered to be told that their 28 year old son was posted missing, believed killed in action. Lieutenant James Cairns had come back from Australia to join up with the RASC in November 1915 and was on attachment with the London Regiment when he was posted missing between 20 March and 4 April. The family had already lost James' younger brother, a gunner with the Canadian forces, in 1917.

What a relief it was then to receive another telegram in May saying that their son was known to be a prisoner of war. But these messages could not keep up with circumstances and James had actually died on 23 April 1918, more than a week before the telegram announcing his salvation was received at the laird's house.

The Western Front was now the primary source of bad news for local families, Periodically however the war at sea was still taking its toll. Despite British domination of the waves since Jutland, a potent German threat remained beneath the waves. The introduction of the convoy system had afforded some protection to merchant fleets from U boats. Losses from the April 1917 peak of 881,000 tons fell to under 300,000 tons in November 1917.[184] However in the early months of 1918 the losses began to rise again.

---

[184] Hough p314

The year had opened with the loss of 19 year old deckhand Alex Corstorphine. He had served his apprenticeship and was another who was employed in the cleek factory. He was from a fishing family however- his father David was skipper/owner of the Steam Drifter *Unity* - and so he joined the Navy. His boat was a captured German steam trawler which was renamed as H.M.T *Gambri*.[185] He was on minesweeping patrol in the Straits of Dover when the *Gambri* struck a mine off the Royal Sovereign Light vessel and blew up. Alex survived the explosion, and managed to swim to a life raft; clinging to it soaking wet and in the middle of winter his life ebbed away. His was the only body found and he was buried in Kilrenny Kirkyard.

In April, Seaman Robert Gardner was one of three men who drowned when the *SS Greynog* on which he was a gunner was torpedoed without warning. The 22 year old, from 2 Rodger Street, had joined up in 1914 - soon after his brother John, who was said to be the first from the town to go on service.

Robert Gardner (in uniform) drowned when his ship was torpedoed.

Finally, William Dunnett (25) engineer on the *SS Benlawers* died when his ship hit a mine in the Irish Channel, killing five of the crew on 12

---

[185] Although his parents had his memorial headstone inscribed with 'HMT Cambrai'

May 1918. He had been recently seen about Anstruther staying at the family home at 6 Union Place and had joined his ill-fated vessel only two weeks before it was hit. His Seaman's Allotment Notes are in the possession of the Kilrenny and Anstruther Burgh Collection. Allotment Notes stipulate that part of a seaman's wages which should be paid to a member of his family. In this case Dunnett instructed that his mother Barbara should be the beneficiary. He first joined the Leith-registered *Benlawers* in May 1914 as 4th Engineer and his mother received £3.10s monthly. By November 1916 he had been made 3rd Engineer on a sister vessel the *Benlomond*, and then was promoted to 2nd Engineer on his original boat. His mother would have received £11.10 s from 1st June - but she did not sign for a penny of that, as by then he was dead. (By coincidence the notice of his death appeared in the local paper on the same date as that of his uncle who had been knocked down and killed by a motorcyclist.)[186]

William Dunnett's mother received a part of his wages
as stipulated in this Allotment Note

Although submarines and mines remained a menace until the end of the

---

[186] EFO 18 July 1918

war William Dunnett was the last local man to die at sea in World War One.

By mid 1918 the war took a decisive turn. Although the German high command knew that to win the war the British had to be defeated it decided in July to launch its next major offensive against the French - and towards Paris. On 15 July the German forces hurled themselves over the river Marne, but were then unexpectedly repulsed by the French in a counter-attack three days later.

These repeated offensives of the Germans meant that the war had in places emerged from the trenches and was being fought in unfamiliar territory. The French commanders had been aware that an attack was coming and had demanded British reinforcements. The second Battle of the Marne as it became known drew upon the resources of five battalions of the Gordon Highlanders - a greater involvement than any other British regiment.

The 4th, 5th and 6th Battalions were sent as part of the 51st division on a hot dusty trip which after three days of travelling decanted them south of the River Marne with no food - so that the troops were officially at least dependent on their emergency rations. To make matters worse they had an exhausting march to take up their position for battle.

(The 6th Black Watch, which was also to be involved in the forthcoming battle suffered similarly. On their trip down they had heard Big Bertha shelling Paris and had the first sight of the American forces. For the French civilians and troops this was their first encounter with Highlanders and in puzzlement they asked if they were Portuguese.)[187]

The counter assault by the Gordons took place on 20th July. Instead of the mud and trenches of Flanders they found themselves blundering about in dense woods - the undergrowth was thick and the Germans opened fire with machine guns from hidden positions. No reconnaissance had been done and officers who were expected to provide the intelligence were cut down at short range by the German defenders. As a result troops got lost, battalions got intermixed and the attack petered out. Day after day the Gordons made an attempt to break through but to no avail. The fluid nature of the offensive and the mixed forces meant for confusion-one day the expected creeping artillery barrage was over 700 yards in front of the attacking forces so that the German were able to regroup

---

[187] Wauchope Vol 2 p189

and repulse the British assault- then the following day the shells fell short so the Gordons found themselves blasted by the French artillery. Still the attack persisted - the 4th Gordons "gained a little ground on July 24th and 25th by short rushes."[188] It was in one of these sapping efforts that Private Wallace Low was killed, the fifth 19 year old to die that year. The apprentice bootmaker worked with his father in James Street a couple of minutes walk from the family home in East Forth Street.[189]

Hungry, hot, lost, and shelled by his own side - it hardly had the making of a military turning point. But the July offensive was meant to sweep the French out of the war and had failed - and had cost the Germans such casualties that the prospect of taking on the British, now augmented by US reinforcements, seemed irreparably set back. In fact it was the Allies who would unleash the decisive offensive.

The impact of the US forces joining the war is viewed differently on either side of the Atlantic. An American historian has argued that the impact of the American presence would have been dissipated if, as the Allied commanders wanted, the US troops were simply used to reinforce British and French positions. The American commander of the American Expeditionary Force, General Pershing had concluded " that the French had no idea how to beat the Germans. The only thing the AEF had seen in the spring of 1918 was mass panic and constant ineptitude."[190] The US it is argued brought not just troops but a more decisive approach to battle - and were able to emulate the stormtrooper assaults of the Germans, using a short massive bombardment and then overwhelming rapid attack, in a way which the lumbering British and French tactics never achieved. The counter argument comes from the British historian Niall Ferguson who has sought to demolish the standpoint from which "It was commonly claimed at the time (and some people still believe it) that the Americans 'won the war". In reality, he argues, the AEF suffered disproportionately large casualties mainly because Pershing still believed in frontal assaults. The US greatest contribution was simply by being there in seemingly inexhaustible numbers at the end of a long and bloody war. "If that was what made the German soldier decide to surrender, it was hardly a triumph of revolutionary tactics."[191]

---

[188] Falls p213

[189] EFO 8 August 1918

[190] Mosier p330

[191] Ferguson pp.312-313

In any case, before the great offensive was launched, the common attrition of war accounted for two local officers. On 31st July Lieutenant George Darsie of the Fife and Forfar Yeomanry died of wounds he had received sometime earlier. He belonged not to the generation of young officers like Thomas Smith but rather was a veteran of the South African war who had gone off to farm in Canada but returned to fight . Towards the end of 1915 he went to the Middle East where he served with the Yeomanry and afterwards with the Camel Corps in Egypt and Palestine.[192] He was then sent to the Western front on attachment to the 8th Btn Cameronians and was caught by small arms fire and died of his wounds at Senlis. It might be expected that his death would occasion extensive mention in the local press.

After all as we have noted the Darsie family was said to be able to trace their lineage back to the Normans and had been present in Anstruther since the 16th century holding prominent positions as elders, baillies and magistrates.

Lieutenant George Darsie

[192] EFO 8 August 1918

His father was a notable man in Anstruther and indeed Fife, being Hon Sheriff Substitute. His sister was at the forefront of raising funds for the war effort, and his brother-in-law was the high profile local solicitor turned soldier Colonel TD Murray. Surprisingly then the coverage in the local paper of Lieut. Darsie's loss was respectful but restrained.

The day after George's death another local officer was killed in action. Lieut. Adam Lindsay was the kind of man who would be expected to be a pillar of local society. He worked in the Clydesdale bank, and had not rushed to the colours at the outbreak of war, joining up in 1916. He lived with his wife in the substantial detached house 'Clifton' on the Pittenweem road. Jeannie gave birth to a daughter on 8 April 1918,[193] and Adam had leave from the 10th Cyclist Btn of the Royal Scots to see his baby. Two months after returning to the front he was dead.

The local paper reported that he had fallen "in the British drive of 1 August."[194] However the decisive push actually took place on 8 August when British and French tanks, backed by Canadian and Australian infantry massed outside Amiens and within four days had retaken the old Somme battleground in what the German commander called "the black day" for the German army.

Thereafter, with the American troops pouring into France, it is clear that the outcome of the war was not really in doubt. However that had been said before and men were still being moblised. In any major city there would be men coming home on leave or being sent home to convalesce, bumping into those going back to the front from leave or after recovering from illness and injury, with a stream of new recruits being thrown into the mix. An appeal was raised in *The Scotsman* for £25,000 to establish a Scottish Union Jack Club in Edinburgh which would provide good sleeping accommodation and meals for the large number of servicemen coming regularly to the city. (An Anstruther woman, Miss E. Rachel Jamieson gave £2 to this fund, one of a series of regular donations.)[195]

Before the war could be said to be over there was fighting still to be done as the Germans tried to find a line to hold - not least so that they could negotiate peace terms from a position of strength. In the last three months of the war local lives were lost in the push for victory. Given the

---

[193] EFO 11 April 1918

[194] EFO 15 August 1918

[195] The Scotsman 20 July 1918. The idea of a military club for those below commissioned rank predated the war. The Union Jack Club was established in London in 1904 by Ethel McCaul a Royal Red Cross Nurse who had served in field hospitals during the Boer War.

fast moving turn of events, as we have seen, official notification did not necessarily keep up with what was happening in the field. Just as important were the eye witness accounts of local men who let families back home know the worst.

Private Shepherd Bissett wrote to say that George Moncrieff, a Gordon Highlander, had been killed by a splinter of shell whilst he was on advanced post duty in front of the trenches. The 20 year old had been a baker with Birrell's in George Street. He was buried where he fell, a cross marking the spot which his family were assured would be replaced by a better one later on. (Although this did not appear to happen as he is commemorated on the Vis-en-Artois memorial which bears the name of 9,000 men with no known grave.)

There could be simple poignancy in the communications from the front. Alex Bissett (Shepherd's cousin) a grocer with Fowlers in Cellardyke was killed in September 1918. His father, a cabinet-maker with Gray and Pringle's, received letters from his comrades assuring him, of course, that his son's death was instantaneous and also enclosing " a very pretty postcard" that was found on the body. Ready for posting it said simply "From Ally to father." A letter was also found near the place where Alex fell. The young soldier, who at 21 had already survived being shot in the head in Palestine, was looking forward to leave soon and to the end of the war.[196]

A fortnight before the end of the war Sergeant James Watt was shot by a sniper. No death can seem fair to a family but to his wife, Thomasina, at home with her four young sons in 3 Bankwell Road the loss of her 31 year old husband must have been so unfair. Sergeant Watt had been at the front for only six weeks. The Anstruther cooper had been in the Black Watch 1st Territorials and was transferred to the Queen's Royal West Surrey Regiment after the outbreak of war. He was retained on home service as a musketry instructor before the draining of reserves and the effort of the British push saw him drafted into active service. Only a few more weeks and he would have been safe.

By now it was clear on the home front that the war was won and the local paper reflected the cruel twist of fate that had spared him throughout the whole of the war only to rob him of his life at the close: "It is a melancholy reflection that he should have had to make the supreme sacrifice just when there is every indication of the war soon coming to an end."[197]

---

[196] EFO 19 September 1918
[197] EFO 7 November 1918

Chapter 8

Beyond the end.

Sadly despite the end of hostilities several more names would be added to the official list of the war dead. Throughout the war it was not only those who had died in combat or captivity who were revered but also those who had succumbed to illness and accident. The first Black Watch Territorial to die as we have seen did not survive the rigours of the training camp. Others succumbed to disease which they might otherwise have caught - 20 year old Robert Parker who used to work in Anstruther Post Office and joined up with the London Postal Rifles died in June 1915 in Bethnal Green Military Hospital of "cerbro-spinal meningitis" (A year later his younger brother also by then 20, was killed with the Black Watch).

Sometimes families had the comfort of burying their sons locally - and even to see them before they died.

The Gourlay family had committed themselves wholeheartedly to the war- five brothers were on naval service. The oldest, George, was on a drifter patrolling the Forth; John was skipper of *HMS Redrift*; the third and fourth sons were engineers on drifters based at Immingham. The youngest was James (23). He had been determined to follow his brothers into naval uniform but had been rejected several times before joining up in January 1916 firstly on a drifter and then on a minesweeper. He was serving on *HMPMS Western Queen* when the war had finished. A week after the Armistice however, his parents in 6 Dove Street, received a telegram saying he had been ill but had got over the worst of it; immediately followed by another warning that he was dangerously ill. He died at South Shields Infirmary with his parents by his side and was buried in Kilrenny with naval honours. All of his brothers were given leave to be at his graveside.

Gourlay had died of pneumonia contracted as a complication arising from the influenza which had laid him low. Spanish flu had first made an impact in June 1918 affecting the German forces more than allied troops. But it was in the autumn and winter that the world wide epidemic (which some say originated in South Africa[198]) prostrated millions. It is estimated that as many died of the flu as had been killed on all sides by the war. Numbers of dead in India alone have been put as high as

---

[198] Keegan p438

16 million. Not surprisingly then it carried away men in uniform - and as they were still on military service they counted towards the military casualties and were commemorated on the war memorials. These included Leading Seaman Robert Thomson (35) of 22 James Street, Cellardyke who died at Plymouth Naval Hospital; and Driver John Wilson (34) of the Black Watch at the Casualty Clearing Station in France.

Another driver, this time in the ASC also fell victim in October. He was Private William Wilson Swan stationed at Retford, West Yorks, the brother of Thomas Swan who had been killed in the first months of the war. The 26 year old had been home to see his bereaved mother only a fortnight earlier and had seemed in perfect health. (Poor Mrs Swan - hers was a long sad war. Almost exactly a year later she had to cope with the death of her son-in-law, who passed away in her home at Chalmers House. 39 year old David Smith had joined up with the Black Watch 3rd Battalion and was then in the Labour Corps. He was wounded in September 1917 and never really recovered.[199])

The effects of the flu swept through Anstruther with the local paper venturing that "very few households or establishments have not felt its effects."[200] In November 1918 all schools were closed for an indefinite period. Fishermen were contracting flu and dying in the nearest port. John Bett (30) who lived in Burnside Terrace came off the *Breadwinner* and Alex Smith (45), Rodger Street, was landed from the *Rothesay Bay*. Both died in hospital in Yarmouth in mid November.[201]

It was to this prostrate community, its people ill in bed, its harbour emptied of boats, its businesses and farms denuded of young men that news of the Armistice came. When it did despite the ravages of flu and pneumonia "there were not wanting signs of jubilation" said the local paper, (which however was not moved to change its usual front page and carried the news only on page 3.[202]) Flags fluttered in the bright November sunshine from the Town Hall, from Waid Academy and were draped from shops and houses. The church bells, silenced for almost all of the war, rang out. A Thanksgiving service was held in the Town Hall. (Elsewhere the celebrations were not quite so douce. In Crail an effigy of the Kaiser was blown up at the aerodrome.[203])

---

[199] EFO 9 October 1919
[200] EFO 7 November 1918
[201] EFO 21 November 1918
[202] EFO 17 November 1918
[203] EFO 17 November 1918

Recruiting was suspended and all outstanding calling up notices were cancelled. People began to prepare for the return of their menfolk. And women. We have no knowledge of how many women from Anstruther volunteered for war service. We know that some had gone off to work in the munitions factory where wages were attractive; one of the Tarvit girls from Cellardyke worked in Singers at Clydebank.

She had a sister who was in the WAAC. The formation of the Women's Army Auxiliary Corps was announced in February 1917 and by the end of March the first draft of women left London for Boulogne. The intention was to employ the women in the Forces Canteens to release men for frontline service. Although they wore uniforms (described as a curious grey brown rather than khaki[204]) and had the insignia WAAC on their shoulders straps just like Army regimental insignia, the military metaphor did not extend to ranks. The privates were called workers and the NCOs were Forewomen. The name was later changed to the Queen Mary's Army Auxiliary Corps and the women soon moved into jobs as clerks, telephonists, and storekeepers.

One of the young Anstruther women who volunteered was Elizabeth Slight Johnson. A former Waid pupil, she grew up in Anstruther at East Green where her father was a rope and sailmaker.[205] She had started work in the Post Office and then moved to take up a post in Glasgow with the Western Union. When the Women's Auxiliary Army Corps was formed she offered her service and eventually arrived in France on 27 December 1917. She died almost exactly one year later, on Christmas Day 1918. Typically such a brief summary is all we know of those lost in the war, but not so in the case of Elizabeth. Not only is she distinguished by the fact that she is the only woman on either of the memorials, uniquely too she was the subject of a book, written in the months immediately following her death *Johnnie of QMAAC* (on account of her being known as Johnnie to her war time comrades , but never apparently to her family or peace time colleagues who called her Liz or Lisbeth) is based largely upon her own recorded words. Elizabeth was a prodigious writer - she kept a diary, wrote hundred of letters to family and friends and submitted poems and articles to the local Anstruther paper.

These seem to have been passed to a family friend who holidayed locally, and who was an author. The overwhelming impression which emerges in the 191 page book is of a decent home-loving girl who seemed

---

[204] Condell and Liddiard p110

[205] In the building which is now The Cellar Restaurant

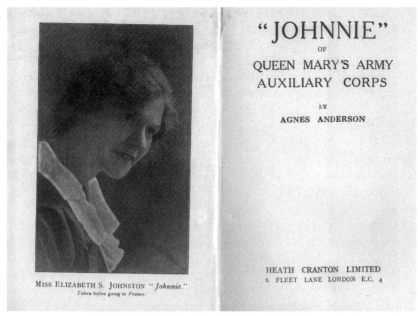

"JOHNNIE"

OF

QUEEN MARY'S ARMY
AUXILIARY CORPS

BY

AGNES ANDERSON

HEATH CRANTON LIMITED
6 FLEET LANE LONDON E.C. 4

MISS ELIZABETH S. JOHNSTON "*Johnnie.*"
Taken before going to France.

The biography of Elizabeth Johnson,
the only woman on the memorials

determined to see the good in everybody. This was strongly evidenced by her Christian beliefs but also in her political ideals. In the early months of the war she wrote: "Aren't these awful times and yet it is a privilege to be alive I think. We are witnessing and taking part in a world wide revolution, for the wheels of the world are revolving, and when they stop, I think the passengers will find themselves all on the same deck. We'll have no more of this stateroom and steerage distinctions; there will be, I feel sure, less of the ermine robe and the coronet and the gulf between the aristocrats and the long-suffering common people will be more easily bridged."[206] She seemed to be particularly exercised by this, noting archly that the men who are now dying for their native land would have been imprisoned if they had taken a short cut over "Lord So and so's pasture land".

On joining up she formed strong bonds with the working class girls from the English cities. Although she maintains a breezy and humorous line, mimicking the mannerisms of speech of her colleagues, nevertheless it is clear that she suffered from bouts of depression and acute homesickness, especially missing her mother. She wrote screeds of pages in her letters

---

[206] Anderson p140

- she was furious when one letter she wrote to her adored mother was returned by the censor, not least because she had written ten pages. In France she made an effort to learn the language, to the extent that she told off a local shopkeeper who had sold oranges to a local woman for '*deux sous*' but then tried to charge the equivalent of sixpence to the British girls. "She nearly had a fit when I strafed her in her own language." Her homesickness lessened and she enjoyed the French countryside, as well as Rouen, the nearest town. She went out shopping with the girls, played hockey for the Camp , (although refusing to play on a Sunday). In addition to her WAAC work she volunteered to work in a hospital treating the war wounded. She seemed to thrive in her work in the Signals department and was a regular correspondent home and to the local paper. She was keen always to report on any contact she had with Anstruther and Cellardyke lads. Out shopping one day in Rouen she bumped into Alex Cunningham (brother of George who had been killed nearly two years earlier.) He had just arrived back in France from being on home leave and was on his way to the front. When visiting Saint Sever cemetery she made a point of seeking out the grave of Davie Watt a 22 year old Anstruther lad who had died of wounds received during the Battle of the Somme. Even then the graves were a place of pilgrimage - she met an English family visiting the graves of two sons. The boys were buried side by side. Despite the killing on an industrial scale each grave was carefully tended. "There was no need to lay flowers on the graves. They are beautifully kept. Davie's was a mass of chrysanthemums, michaelmas daisies and lovely begonias."[207]

Within weeks Elizabeth would be buried in the same cemetery. Looking at her date of death the first assumption is that she had succumbed to the flu epidemic which swept the world at the end of 1918. Indeed she was hospitalised at the beginning of December, but recovered thanks, she said, to chicken broth and chicken dinners and milk puddings and real milk; not to mention the presents of pears, apples, chocolate, grapes and cake with which she was inundated. Although at least one of her Signals colleagues died in the same ward, Elizabeth was discharged from hospital and was well enough to be back at work for Christmas. She went on night duty on 24 December carrying her breakfast rations, saying she intended going to Rouen for the morning service in the cathedral. After coming off duty at 8 am she made her way into town but instead of going to the cathedral,went to the empty Church of Saint Ouen. A caretaker offered her a light as she climbed the tower but she declined, saying she knew the way as she had been there before. He was the last

---

[207] Anderson p149

114

person she spoke to - by early afternoon she was found by two American soldiers lying on the roof of the chapel, having apparently fallen from the tower.[208]

Elizabeth Johnston's grave in St Sever Cemetry.

The circumstances of her death are mysterious. Why did she not go to the Christmas service? Why on a raw winter day and having just recovered from the flu would she spend so much time at the top of the tower? She was up there alone for over four hours. According to one of her friends who had been up to the top the space was so restricted that she would have had to be sitting on a balustrade leaning back against the tower. The consensus of opinion at the time was that she lost her balance, weakened as she was by the effects of the flu and lack of sleep, and fell the 80 feet to the roof below. The book which she had taken up with her was found a few yards from her body. As to why she chose to go up this tower- well, according to a young soldier with whom she was friendly the two of them had climbed the tower on the 17 December, but mist obscured the view and she had told him then that she wanted to go up again sometime.

This soldier, Donald Cameron, a Canadian Highlander, had only met Elizabeth on Armistice Day but was moved to make a dramatic gesture at her funeral. Knowing of her profound sense of Scottishness he replaced the Union Flag which was draped over her coffin with a Saltire Flag which he had somehow acquired. He provided an eye witness account of the ceremony in Saint Sever cemetery. South African Highlanders in Atholl tartan provided the firing party and 60 girls from the Signals Corps, a dozen lady officers, as well as 42 officers and men from a nearby camp were gathered. This was gratefully received by her family, as none of them were present - but not for the want of trying. A telegram had arrived in Anstruther at about 9 am on 26th December saying Elizabeth had met with a serious accident. Later another arrived saying simply "Elizabeth passed away on Christmas afternoon." (These were not official despatches but were sent by Madge Deans, a homespun Welsh girl who was Elizabeth's closest friend.) Her brother and two sisters set off the following day determined to get to France, even though they seemed not to have any passports. When they got to London the War Office refused to grant them permits to attend a funeral, saying it was against their rules and regulations.

Back home her bereft mother must have recalled one of Elizabeth's earlier letters in which she sought to reassure her that "the chances of anything serious befalling a W.A.A.C. are very remote indeed, in fact, nigh impossible."

For those who were spared to come back demobilisation took place slowly with a cumbersome and often apparently unjust system which could mean men who had given long service remaining in uniform whilst those with short service but a guarantee of a job getting home more quickly.

Prisoners of war trickled back with detailed accounts of their ordeals. Private William Birrell of the 6th Black Watch whose parents lived in Shore Street Anstruther had the kind of story with a local twist which the paper relished. We knew of course that he had ended up in hospital and that with the benefit of Red Cross parcels was faring reasonably well, compared to others. On his return however he was able to give details of his capture. He had been caught by a heavy bombardment at Bapaume in March 1918. He was still unscathed however when the enemy overran his position. But as the Germans pulled him out of the trench he apparently fainted and when he came to he found himself lying on the parapet of the trench with bullets whistling around him. Whilst he had lain there unconscious he had been hit and severely wounded - but he was able to crawl into a shell hole for safety. Eventually a German Red Cross man crawled out to him, dressing his wounds. Still he could not get to safety and remained in the shell hole for two days and nights until he was taken behind the German lines and to a dressing station. Thereafter "after a little coffee of burnt barley and soup made of bean powder"[209] he was dumped into a bed with another prisoner - who incredibly was Private Henry Boyter of Cellardyke. Both eventually were sent to Russian Poland where they were well enough treated but had to subsist on watery soup and a slice of bread daily.

Those who were not wounded seemed to fare worse. Private George Cormack had been a cleek finisher in Anderson's factory. He was captured in April 1917 and for seven days received no food except some bread and water. He was then pressed into service in the German reserve trenches where the prisoners suffered many casualties from shell fire, and the the rest were on the verge of starvation. Their lives, it was said, were saved by parcels from home.[210]

This kind of account was commonplace. Private William Leslie of Kirk Wynd Anstruther and, like Cormack, a Black Watch soldier, was captured in April 1918. He found that hard labour under shell fire was the norm - repairing roads, making railway lines and ammunition dumps. The physical demands and the inadequate diet saw him hospitalised. Even that brought only temporary relief as the hospital took a direct hit from an artillery shell and was wrecked with 12 patients being killed.[211]

Such conditions made the prisoners susceptible to disease. Sergeant James Smith who was captured in March 1918 died in Prussia of dropsy in August 1918 (although the information did not come back to Anstruther until after the end of the war). The 30 year old former postal worker had joined up on the day war had broken out serving in the 1/7 Black Watch transport.

Surviving PoWs were valued as a potential source of specific news of missing men. The parents of Corporal C Elder 2nd Battalion Royal Scots placed an advert in the paper appealing for returned PoWS to contact them at their home in East Pitcorthie if they had any information about their son who had gone missing in April 1918.

Of course the news could confirm worst fears rather than dispel dread. Another Elder, this time 2nd Lieutenant James Elder, 6th Black Watch

---

[209] EFO 10 January 1919

[210] EFO 24 January 1919

[211] EFO 3 January 1919

had been missing since 21st March 1918. As he had been attached latterly to the 7th Black Watch, the local battalion, his parents in High Street Anstruther anxiously sought out returning POWs who had to break the news that their 23 year old son had in fact been killed that day. The end of war had brought the end of hope.

Chapter 9

A Time of Reckoning

The end of the war also brought a time of reckoning. The men who fought and died needed to be acknowledged for their sacrifice. But so too did those who had fought and lived. They deserved special consideration for their willingness to die; their loss of earnings and the continued hardship and lack of official recognition which many felt was due to them. The community was capable of doing both of course but from time to time tempers frayed with accusations that one or other - the dead or the living were being neglected.

There had been an acknowledgement for some time that a memorial to those who had served and in particular to those who had died should be erected once the war had come to a close.

In the dark days of 1917 when it seemed the war might go on forever Provost Porter of Anstruther Wester had made a melancholy and emotional speech to the Town Council. He was clearly moved by the death of Baillie Brodie's son. He did not believe that he would live to see the end of the war but he hoped whoever his successors might be they would see that the memories of the Burgh's heroes were not blotted out or forgotten. "Rolls of honour on a piece of parchment were all very good' he said (although his own proposal for a roll of honour had never materialised in Anstruther) but he considered that "a monument should be erected in memory of the dear brave young fellows who had paid the last penalty of a cruel war."[212]

Provost Porter did live to see the end of the war and renewed his call for a memorial, just before Christmas 1918. As ever his views were forthright and determined by two consistent priorities - to avoid any drain on the public purse and to ensure that Anstruther Wester was favoured by any outcome which involved dealings with the other burghs. So whilst he hoped that the monument would be of a nature that would worthily commemorate the memories of the poor fellows who had sacrificed their lives he accepted that "Its shape and magnitude of course would depend on the sum that could be raised" (by public subscription). Then more controversially he suggested that whilst Anstruther Easter and Cellardyke might combine with Anstruther Wester, whatever was decided Billowness

---

[212] CBO 15 October 1917

would have to be the site.[213] And so the basis for a conflict that would rage for two years was laid.

Billowness is a headland at the western extremity of Anstruther - almost as far from Cellardyke as it is possible to be without finding yourself in the neighbouring town of Pittenweem. (It has a colourful past. Skeletons and old burial sites have been exposed which were said to be the remains of Roman soldiers attacked at what was once known as Chesterhill Knowe or, just as likely, of native defenders against invasion; and lepers were banished from the town to die there. Crowds flocked there for open air preaching from what is still called Johnnie Doo's pulpit. By the early part of the 20th century it had been incorporated into the new little golf course - of which Provost Porter was an enthusiastic supporter.)

The proposal drew an immediate negative reaction - Baillie Brodie, of Anstruther Easter said he was in favour of a joint memorial but considered Billowness an out of the way place for the monument.[214] Provost Black for Kilrenny rejected the idea of a joint memorial given that "the site had been fixed upon" and illustrated his determination to have Cellardyke recognised by saying that he had already examined sketches, sent up from London no less, for a separate memorial.[215]

The dispute was borne out of old rivalries but also opened up fissures in the way local people wanted to acknowledge the war. The letters pages of the local press grew heated. A strong body of opinion argued for the memorial to be utilitarian not sentimental. In particular a letter calling for the construction of a bridge across the Dreel Burn (the traditional demarcating line between the Anstruthers) running from the end of Castle Street to the Esplanade, was favoured. The author, signing himself as Old Anster Boy, thought it could be adorned with lights bearing the Coats of Arms of the two Anstruther Burghs and a roll of honour at either end.[216] One correspondent, backing this scheme said "we have far too many useless monuments in our country already"[217] Encouraged by the positive response the anonymous originator of the idea wrote to say that he had discussed the design with a bridge builder in Glasgow and furthermore he was prepared to undertake collection of subscriptions in

---

[213] EFO 19 December 1918

[214] EFO 19 December 1918

[215] EFO 19 December 1918

[216] EFO 14 February 1918

[217] EFO 7 March 1919

the West of Scotland if the Council should back his scheme.[218]

A joint meeting was held to try to resolve the dispute which now had to consider three things - should there be a joint memorial at all; if so where should it be (Cellardyke was promoting a rival location at Blyth's Park) and what form should it take? Sir Robert Lorimer the renowned architect at Kellie Castle should be approached to resolve the dispute it was decided.[219]

Church memorials were in place long before the official town memorials.

The municipal memorials were not however the only recognition of sacrifice. The names of the dead and also often of those who served were to be honoured in smaller tributes throughout the three burghs - in churches; schools; masonic lodge and even the golf club. Anstruther Parish Church memorial was to be a modest affair - estimated to cost £320 of which £10 would come from the Women's Guild. The memorial at Chalmers United Free Church was altogether grander. It was reckoned that 158 members of the congregation had served - 63 army; 67 navy;

---

[218] EFO 14 March 1919
[219] EFO 21 March 1919

23 other forces. These were all men of course. The Reverend Urquhart asked the congregation if they objected to leaving out the names of women in service and it " was unanimously agreed that this should be so as there were so many departments in which women had been employed in connection with the war."[220]

The Chalmers Church memorial was on a significantly greater scale than the parish church. The 28 members of the congregation amongst the fallen were to be honoured on stained glass windows which were to be designed by James Ballantine FSA Scot at a cost of £500. Six lights in the window would variously depict youth, war on land, war on sea and victory. Those who survived were to be commemorated on brass tablets costing £25. A service to dedicate the new memorial was held on May 30th 1920 to which the Revd Urquhart, who had by that time been called to Greenock, returned to officiate.

David Brown – 'the Silent Postie'
fought through from 1914-1919

It was not just honouring the dead that exercised the town but also those

---

[220] EFO 18 March 1919

who had survived. The scale of the conflict was such that as in every community ordinary men were returning, who had done something extraordinary. Men who would have been locally known from school had disappeared, and then re-emerged some years later with a depth of experience which could scarcely be imagined and which often they did not talk about. The famously taciturn Cellardyke postie David Brown had already served in the Boer War, and was one of the first to join up on the outbreak of war in 1914. His first narrow escape with death was when a shell shattered the dixie in which he was making tea for his company. He was then wounded in the thigh during the Battle of the Aisne and was shipped home. His convalesence was brief and by the end of November 1914 he was back at the front. He fought throughout the war and even served in Afghanistan before returning to Cellardyke to resume his quiet duties as the 'Silent Postie', with no ceremony or fuss.

Several individuals now returning had distinguished themselves in the war and some ceremony was called for.

The most prestigious awards won by local men were of the Distinguished Service Order (instituted in 1886 for officers of Major and below who distinguished themselves on active service) or the Distinguished Conduct Medals (instituted during the Crimean war) for NCOs and men. The First World War saw the creation of new awards the Military Cross (instituted December 1914) as a reward for gallantry for junior officers in the army and from 1916 the Military Medal to NCOs and men.[221]

Presentation of medals won by those in the ranks did not always match the glittering investitures at the Buckingham Palace enjoyed by officers. When Drummer Harry Bowman, won the Military Medal in 1916 it was presented to him by Provost Readdie when he was home on leave in Feb 1918, the ceremony taking place in the interval of the pantomime Puss in Boots!

Bowman served with the 1/7 Black Watch and during the Battle of the Somme they were in action in High Wood on 30 July 1916. Most of his comrades had fallen and "amidst heavy fire of shot and shell" he brought in a mortally wounded Pittenweem soldier. Bowman, who came from a fishing family in John Street, (his grandfather had been a whaler in the Arctic) was a painter with D Walker before the war. He was the young apprentice who had been reported monosyllabically giving evidence at

---

[221] Fowler et al p37

a fatal accident inquiry in 1914, the only previous time he had his name in the paper.

Many local men did not receive their medals until well after the end of the war. A grand presentation ceremony took place as late as December 1919. It was a far more appropriate occasion than that encountered by Harry Bowman. Eleven men from Cellardyke and three from Anstruther were presented with their medals by the local provosts, in front of an audience of more than 300 demobilised soldiers and sailors. The local paper enthused that "seldom if ever has Anstruther Town Hall presented such a dazzling spectacle" as the town honoured the men on their return.

*Skipper John Hughes was decorated for rescuing
hundreds of Italian soldiers in the Adriatic*

Five of the sailors won the Serbian Gold Medal in recognition of the prominent part played by Cellardyke men in the Adriatic. Skipper John Hughes, of the drifter *Evening Star* received the DSC as well as the Serbian Gold Medal for his part in the sinking of an Austrian submarine as well as for the rescue of 300 soldiers on an Italian transport ship which had been cut in two by a mine in the Mediterranean.[222] James Wilson a Cellardyke fisherman who had been taken prisoner was back home to receive his medal; also there was Skipper David Watson to receive three decorations from the Italian, French and Serbian authorities.

A local grocer from Cunzie Street, John Simpson came forward to collect his Military Medal. As a private in the Machine Gun Corps he had performed heroically when, in the face of heavy machine gun fire, he had recovered ammunition for his sections guns from an evacuated position " under his own initiative" (a telling phrase in itself as private soldiers in the British Army were renowned for doing only what they were ordered to do). The same day he had again braved heavy enemy fire to bring in a wounded and helpless man and then had rounded his day of glory by surprising a party of the enemy with bombs "and did great execution" setting a magnificent example of courage according to his citation.[223]

Not everyone who was decorated was presented with their medals that night. Sergeant W Taylor of the Argyll and Sutherland Highlanders (who was not demobilised until April 1919) won his DCM when after being reported missing he returned after several days behind the enemy lines with "valuable information on the disposition of enemy positions."[224] Prior to the war William Taylor whose home was in East Green had been a hairdresser in Glasgow.

Lance Corporal A Budd was another who won the DCM and was later promoted to Sergeant. He was in the Tank Corps and was attacking the enemy in early spring 1918 when on top of the enemy trenches his tank received a direct hit which wounded most of the crew. Budd kept the Germans at bay by throwing bombs at them and then got the wounded men to safety.[225]

The guest of honour and speaker at the glittering presentation ceremony in December 1919 was himself highly decorated and an interesting character. Lt Col TD Murray was a local man who had been educated at Waid Academy and then St Andrews University. Prior to the war he had been a prominent local solicitor and was another to give substance to Kitchener's view of the Territorials by becoming Town Clerk of

---

[222] (The account in EoFR 17 August 1916 says that a DCM was awarded. But the account of the ceremony of presentation in EFO 18 December 1919 notes a DSC)

[223] EFO 19 September 1918

[224] EFO 10 April 1919

[225] EFO 4 April 1918

Earlsferry as well as commanding the local contingent of the 7th Black Watch. He was over 40 when he was given command of the 8th Hampshire battalion and was sent to Gallipoli and then Egypt. But as a former Black Watch officer he offered himself for service in France even at a reduced rank so long as he could serve with the 1/4 Black Watch. In late 1916 for his leadership at Thiepval he was awarded the DSO. He was a larger than life character - a keen mountaineer, a bagpipe player, and an expert on bulldogs. He loved to entertain and after his marriage to Georgina (the daughter of Sheriff Darsie and Princess Titaua Marama) they added a ballroom to Johnston Lodge. He was renowned for his plain speaking and his enthusiasm for sport which may explain the thrust of his speech to the massed ranks of the veterans. Not for him the gushing or jingoistic tributes. He knew too much from active service; yet he was of the officer class and spoke for that breed apart.

"I often wonder how you stuck it out. The soldier had not the faintest idea of what patriotism meant. He knew the Boche was a fellow he had to beat and knew it meant that he had to stick it until he had beaten him".

This was an important point - not only do we now wonder at how men could have endured the conditions of trench war and the appalling carnage and likelihood of death, it was an issue of the time. As early as 1915 the German commanders had realised that a breakthrough was unlikely and that the only way to win the war would be through taking the enemy beyond the limit of endurance. This was not just attrition but also sapping the soldiers and public belief that any military gain could be achieved in return for the horrific losses. As we have seen doubts about whether a breakthrough could be achieved, or at acceptable cost, were readily aired in Anstruther in 1917.

Commentators have advanced various explanations as to why the men put up with war - such as the deferential class structure of Edwardian society. One said that the British soldier was motivated by a combination of patriotism and the fear of the consequences of disobeying orders and ultimately obeyed them out of a combination of "habit, social deference ... personal loyalty and respect."[226]

Col. Murray had come to his own somewhat idiosyncratic view as to why the ordinary soldier could put up with the horror of war and the privations of trench life: "I really believe that what made him stick it was his sense of humour and love of sport because the minute he was

---

[226] Simpson in Liddle ed pp150

out of the line, out came the football."[227] Football? It seems scarcely credible that football could have bolstered morale sufficiently to cope with the physical and psychological depredations of the prolonged struggle. But there is no doubt that sport and football in particular was passionately pursued by troops once out of the firing line. For the British it was an obsession.[228] It was said that even in Wellington's time that it was a commonplace recreation. And whilst General Haig thought it was a waste of energy when troops could have been better occupied in sleeping or relaxing, the game was actually made compulsory in the hard winter of 1917 and every platoon was provided with a regulation ball.[229] (Some were already well equipped in that respect. As well as the usual consignment of socks, cigarettes, chocolate, and candles, one parcel from Scotland in March 1916 also contained fourteen pairs of football boots, three balls and two pumps.[230] However this was a special case as it was sent by John McCartney manager of Heart of Midlothian to the 16th Btn Royal Scots in which many of his players were serving.)

There is no doubt that football was as important to the Fife men as any other. One local Royal Scots private marvelled at the incongruity of a day when he watched ten enemy aircraft overhead with about 20 guns firing at them whilst on the field below a football match was being played and in another corner of the field the regimental band was playing selections of the latest music.[231]

It could become even more surreal. Before he was killed, Private George Cunningham wrote home to tell of in his astonishment at walking into a village where a football match was being played only to hear the shout "Come on Anster Rangers" particularly as it was an English Regiment on the field - but the fan was, it turns out, from Pittenweem.[232]

Certainly for the local men demobilised after the war football was a passion. In 1919 an Anstruther branch of the Comrades of the Great War was established. By April 1919 it had 58 members, by the following month 200. Forming a football team was one of its first preoccupations. In May it played a match against the Crail Aerodrome team on Waid Academy park (winning 3-0).[233]

---

[227] EFO 18 December 1919

[228] Ferguson p353

[229] Winter D. pp155-6

[230] Alexander p129

[231] CBO 18 October 1917

[232] EoFR 25 May 1916

[233] EFO 22 May 1919

These were not always friendlies - the local paper was moved to observe that "it is difficult at times to distinguish whether a mill fight is in progress or a football match when present at the games played under the east Fife football league" and warned that spectators were overstepping the mark when "deliberately interfering with the players."[234]

By September 1919 the Comrades had resolved to resuscitate the old Anstruther Rangers Football Club. There was goodwill towards the ex-combatants - the Waid Academy Governors agreed to the free use of their park every evening after 5pm and afternoons on Wednesday and Saturday.[235] The veterans were irked however that that there was no ground that they could call their own. It added to the sense that they were being neglected and indeed that the town was more preoccupied with raising funds to commemorate the dead than to acknowledge the efforts of those who had returned.

In Anstruther one of the arguments put forward at a public meeting to discuss the war memorial was for a public park rather than for a memorial out at Billowness. Certainly there was sympathy for the demobilised men, including from those who had lost sons in the war with Baillie Brodie finding it "strange that the boys who had been fighting for Scotland could not get an inch of ground they could really call their own."[236]

However the primary purpose of the Comrades (whose membership was over 400 by the end of 1919) was not recreation. It was to "perpetuate the memory of the fallen, to watch and safeguard the interests of ex-members of the forces, to press the claims of discharged men and to secure adequate pensions."[237] Opening up premises in Shore Street they became a formidable force in the town.

They had complaints about the non payment of gratuities (£20 for a private, £28 for a Lance Corporal). They were also aggrieved at the low level of these rewards and in June 1919 a resolution was moved that "the gratuities awarded to men of the services on demobilisation were totally inadequate, keeping in view the fact that the men referred to were the means of freeing Britain from Prussian militarism."

---

[234] EFO 27 November 1919

[235] EFO 25 September 1919

[236] EFO 4 September 1919

[237] EFO 17 April 1919

Their grievance at not being given their due was heightened by the celebrations being prepared for Saturday 19 July 1919 which was officially declared as the day for the Celebration of Peace. Local ex-servicemen protested that they were not acknowledged or included in the programme of events. The editorial in the local paper protested that the men had not been forgotten and feebly suggested that the organising committee had felt that to call on the soldier and sailor to do another bit would be against their wishes. It noted ruefully however that "leaving the demobilised men alone nowadays is like holding a red rag up to a bull" and suggested therefore that it was not too late to include the local branch of the comrades in the preparations and "give them a prominent share in the celebration of the peace which after all was only made possible by their sufferings and privations."[239]

(Some Comrades Associations elsewhere objected to the celebrations being held at all given the amount of money that was being spent on them).[240]

The celebrations in Anstruther went ahead nevertheless and the local paper employed the kind of plush language which was reserved for these kind of occasions. " It was truly a day of national rejoicing. A people more addicted to self glorification than we might with perfect accuracy have described it as Victory day ."

The events were due to span twelve hours. They were to start with a short service in the morning in various schools, resuming in the afternoon with a fancy dress procession and then the focus would be on Waid Park with sports, a baby show and dancing concluded with a bonfire at Billowness.

Events did not quite go to plan. Firstly the services in the school were cancelled due to cleaning, (proving that the powers of the janitorial staff have long been exercised). The events in the park did get underway although children could get free cups of tea only if they brought their own cups. However each would be delighted to be presented with a brand new 1918 penny - little realising however that these were a substitute for intended medals which had not been obtained on time.

As night fell the paper delighted in the splendid view of the illuminations on both sides of the Forth with the bonfires on Berwick Law and Arthur's

---

[239] EFO 17 July 1919
[240] EFO 3 July 1919

Seat clearly visible. However the folks across there would have looked in vain for a reciprocal sighting of the Anstruther illuminations. The expected firework display had to be abandoned as owing to the railway strike the fireworks were not delivered, although a few desultory rockets were set off. To cap it all when town folk wandered out to Billowness for the bonfire at the allotted time they found only charred remains - "the beacon had already been set ablaze by some over impatient youths."[241]

---

[241] EFO 24 July 1919

Chapter 10

Together we stand, divided we recall.

The national peace celebrations did not bring an end to local hostilities as the furore over the war memorials continued. At times they resembled treaty negotiations. First one side would withdraw saying that the plan for a joint memorial was dead whilst another came forward with new proposals. These were not local politicians playing at local politics - they seemed to be faithfully representing the partisan nature of their communities. When the senior school children of Cellardyke school advertised a fund-raising concert for the memorial the paper was obliged to print a detailed explanation of what would happen to any money raised. Should it be agreed to have a joint memorial then the proceeds would go to the construction of it; should however the two burghs decide to act independently then the money would go to the Cellardyke memorial; and if there was no public memorial then the funds would be reserved for erecting an appropriate school memorial

In what may have been a public test of the expected outcome the folk of Cellardyke turned up for the show and those of Anstruther stayed away. A Dyker wrote sarcastically to the press "I had the pleasure of counting 4 Anster folk. That was good for Anster seeing there were 620 people in the hall... yet they expect the Dykers to let the memorial be placed in Anster."[242]

Opinion was hardening in Cellardyke with a strong view that "the place with the most fallen belonging to it should have a voice in the selection of a site." Anstruther Wester remained implacably fixed on Billowness.

In Anstruther Easter there was still a current in favour of a functional form. The rector of Waid Academy noted the need for communal sports grounds and thought that acquiring and dedicating these would serve as a memorial.[243]

Given the sensitivity of the issue with men still dying late into 1919 from the privations of service, the forthright manner in which some opinions were expressed was remarkable. One local complained that "Monuments hover and loom over us. Nearly always hideous monuments. Often I think they only serve but one purpose - they make capital perches

---

[242] EFO 17 July 1919
[243] EFO 29 May 1919

for loungers and loafers."[244]

Another drew attention to the appeal for funds for blinded soldiers and compared it to the "futility and one might say waste of asking people to contribute large sums to erect memorials to the fallen heroes."[245] But for most people it was not a case of whether there should be a memorial, but how many and where. For a brief time it seemed that out of deference to his reputation the proposal of Sir Robert Lorimer might unite the burghs. After all he had been commissioned to restore Dunrobin Castle and Dunblane Cathedral and had been knighted for his work prior to the war. He retained a willingness to take on local commissions such as designing the war memorial for little Carnbee and the Communion Table at Cellardyke Church. His report dismissed Billowness which, although having the benefit of being visible from land and sea, was too far removed from the life of the town and too far west to form a combined memorial (saying in effect what others had said since the site was first proposed by Provost Porter).

He favoured a site at the intersection of the Crail and St Andrews Roads. The advantage of this site was that it was "central; would improve the traffic conditions if rounded; and by raising it on a terrace would be sufficiently retired and have the character a memorial should have."[246] He even drew up plans of what the memorial should look like.

But local enmities were now well entrenched and the plan was rejected at a public meeting in Cellardyke. (Rebuffed, Sir Robert Lorimer left well alone and took on the less demanding task of designing the magnificent Scottish National War Memorial in Edinburgh Castle.)

The traffic management element of his plans however caught the imagination of some in Anstruther Easter who debated whether the Buckie House should not be demolished to provide a site and at the same time remove a dangerous corner. (The Buckie House, a 17th century building decorated with shells by the eccentric slater and joiner Alexander Batchelor in the mid 19th century, survived several subsequent attempts to clear it away and still brings traffic to a halt to this day).

The clock had ticked around to November 1919 and still no public

---

[244] EFO 12 June 1919
[245] EFO 26 June 1919
[246] EFO 17 April 1919

memorial had been commissioned. The first Armistice Day was observed; in Anstruther two rockets were fired from the harbour to alert the town of the 11th hour having struck. Workmen engaged in repairing boats ceased work and "it was obvious that the King's recommendation was carried out in every respect... There was very little traffic on the streets and roads, but most of the motors and other vehicles drew up to a standstill."[247]

Disputes over the siting and nature of war memorials drew strong opinions in neighbouring communities too. In Pittenweem every proposed site had its detractors. If placed in the churchyard it was felt that it would be overshadowed by other, more impressive, tombstones; but erecting it in the recreation park would desecrate the memory of the fallen. The bereaved were often vociferous in these debates. Mr and Mrs Lindsay let it be known that if the Pittenweem memorial was sited in Market Place then they wanted their son's name omitted. In St Monans Barbara M. Allen, a sailor's widow, objected to the monument being placed outside her home at Braehead. "We have a good remembrance of sorrow inside the house when we have got the still voice and the vacant chair without placing a memorial a few yards from our door", she complained.[248]

By 1920 it was clear that there were going to be two memorials for Anstruther and Cellardyke. Committees were now busy trying to raise funds, commission designs and gather the names of the dead who were to be commemorated on them.

A Scottish Advisory Committee on War Memorials had been established and had held an exhibition at the National Gallery in Edinburgh to assist those commissioning memorials. As well as a representative sample of existing monuments it also displayed designs and models of new works from Scottish artists.[249]

However despite grand talk of designs being sent up from London, commissions stayed within Fife. For Anstruther a St Andrews architect, CF Anderson, was asked to submit designs and, although they met with little enthusiasm, by April 1920 it was formally decided that the site should be Billowness and the design should be in the nature of "a tower or other monumental character".[250] He was also the designer of the St

---

[247] EFO 11 November 1919
[248] EFO 18 March 1920
[249] EFO 15 May 1915
[250] EFO 19 April 1920

Monans memorial (which was to be placed at Braehead despite Mrs Allen's objections) and the Crail memorial which takes the form of fine pillars and gates to the church with the names of 41 men inscribed on bronze panels.

Meanwhile the Kilrenny war memorial (encompassing Cellardyke) was commissioned from a Kirkcaldy architect Mr Murdoch and the site was chosen - Kilrenny Common. Although the location occasioned no immediate public comment it clearly led to rumblings of discontent. Allowing that Kilrenny is properly the name of the burgh and Cellardyke can formally be named as Nether Kilrenny the reality is that most of those who had died came from the Cellardyke streets close to the shore. A landward monument tucked away in Kilrenny Common would have no more presence or visibility to the Cellardyke people than one on Billowness.

Having established where and how the fallen should be commemorated the next vexatious issue was of establishing who was to be acknowledged. No roll of honour had been kept up to date of those serving from the communities in the various branches of the services. Nor had a record of the dead been maintained. Although Cellardyke had claimed that it had sacrificed most in the war, the Town Clerk was unable to say how many had been lost from each burgh.

However there were sources available. Rolls of honour and lists of the dead had been variously drawn up for churches, the schools, the Golf Club, and the Masonic Lodge. These could form the basis for the public memorials and these names were advertised in the paper and relatives were asked to come forward with any which had been omitted.

The upshot of this approach is that names which might be expected to appear are absent from the memorial and others are included somewhat out of the blue.

The Anstruther Easter parish church tablet has 17 names - one of whom, Joseph Aitken, is not on the town memorial. The Cellardyke Church communion table designed by Sir Robert Lorimer has 23 names. Yet not all these appear on the Cellardyke memorial. Four were parishioners who lived in Anstruther and appear on the Billowness memorial but a further three others are not on either of the burgh memorials. Robert Wallace, for instance, had left his wife and four children behind in 64

James Street and was to see service in Dardanelles as 2nd Hand of HM Trawler *Fisher Boy*. He was still there in October 1917 when he died on a hospital ship and was buried in East Mudros Military Cemetery. Why did neither his wife Janet or his father Robert, also of course a fisherman, who lived
in Burnside Terrace, ensure his name was on the main memorial?

The Kilrenny Parish Church memorial of parishioners lost in the war lists 15 names. Again three are not on the memorial including Deck Hand David Reid who was lost from HM Trawler *Robert Smith* on 20 July 1917. The 44 year old who lived with his wife and three children at 20 Shore Street Cellardyke was reported in the press as being well known and respected in the burgh. If so why is he not on the memorial?

The Tarvits provide a miniature case study of omission and inclusion. The Kilrenny church memorial includes three Tarvits - James of 1/7 Black Watch; and Deck Hands William and another James. The Cellardyke Parish Church table also has a James Tarvit. Yet there is only one Tarvit on the Cellardyke burgh memorial. This is William, a former cleek finisher in Baillie Brodie's factory who became a stoker in the RNRT. Twice he escaped with his life after being run down whilst on patrol, the shock of which saw him invalided out of the service. He died in June 1918 of consumption, aged 23. Whilst he appears on the the memorial he is not recorded on the Commonwealth War Graves Commission records perhaps because he was discharged before he died.

Conversely James Tarvit does figure in the CWGC records but not on the memorial. He joined the 1/7 Black Watch but subsequently was transferred to the Railway Operating Division of the Royal Engineers. As a sapper he had been home on leave in January 1917, but was gassed at the front on 9 May and was brought to Manorcourt Hospital at Folkestone where he died on 20 June 1917 aged 27.

Both of these men had a father called James. However they are not brothers. William was the second son of his father who was still on active service in 1918. It was his sister who worked at Singers and the other was in the WAAC. His two brothers were also on naval service. Sapper Tarvit was older than William and was the youngest son of a father who had died at the naval base in 1914. (It is possible then that the remaining James on the Kilrenny church memorial is his father.)

It is inexplicable that Sapper Tarvit should be overlooked. The local paper had recorded his visit home on leave, a death notice had been advertised in its columns and his passing away had been carried in the news pages. He was commemorated by his church and yet he is omitted from the official town memorial.

The opportunity was there to ensure his name was recorded. On 11 August 1921 the list of the names of the men (and one woman) to be inscribed on the Anstruther memorial were advertised on the front page of the *East Fife Observer*. By 1 September three further names had been added - one was Robert Carmichael a signaller in the Highland Light Infantry of which no mention had been made previously.[251]

Another late addition was a regular soldier Private James Gilmour of C Company the 1st Battalion Black Watch. To know what had happened to him requires recalling the opening events of the war. The British were then pursuing the retreating German army as it withdrew from the gains it had made at the end of August 1914. On 14 September the 1st Battalion were ordered to attack German troops who were holding the old Roman road Chemin des Dames on the crest of chalk hills by the River Aisne. It was not clear if they were a rearguard of the retreating army; or the entire army itself, dug in. Historically as it turns out it was the whole army - as 14 September 1914 marks the day of the beginning of trench warfare. The German commander had ordered the withdrawal should fall back to the Aisne and "there the lines so reached will be fortified and defended".[252]

Not surprisingly then the Black Watch attack foundered and by nightfall and in the pouring rain the Scottish soldiers were throwing up the "first spadefuls of that long line that was to stretch from Switzerland across France to the sea."[253] At daybreak C Company were sent to see if the Germans were still there - and this was affirmed by a hail of heavy fire. Private Gilmour died the following day, 16 September 1914.

The significance of his unremarked and only belatedly acknowledged death seems not to have been appreciated. For it is Private Gilmour who was in fact the first Anstruther man to die in the First World War. This distinction has always been accorded to Petty Officer Frederick Blunsdon.

---

[251] The records of the Commonwealth War Graves Commission show a Private RH Carmichael who died with the Cameronians (Scottish Rifles) on 12.5.1918
[252] Keegan p133
[253] Wauchope Vol. 1 pp. 13-14

Even when his father died in 1918 the local paper had him down as "father of Fred, the first local victim of the war."[254] Yet Fred died in November 1914, eight weeks after James Gilmour.

Anstruther War Memorial at Billowness

On Christmas Day 1921 the joint Anstruther memorial was ready to be unveiled and dedicated. The dignitaries for the event included the local MP Sir Alex Sprott and Sir Ralph Anstruther who provided the address in the Town Hall, where the ex-servicemen led by Lt Col TD Murray had assembled. Sir Ralph had recalled standing in the same hall in the early days of a war which had come like a bolt from the blue. The determination to resist the Germans, he said, was coupled however with a belief that it would all be over in a few weeks or months at the most. What had come to the rescue of the nation, when the scale of the conflict had to be endured, was patriotism - love of country made the most tremendous sacrifice possible (thereby unwittingly directly contradicting the opinion of Col Murray who had dismissed any notion of patriotism amongst those who, in the trenches, were actually called upon to make the sacrifice). And so to Billowness for the unveiling. The architect had

[254] EFO 14 March 1918

designed a Scottish baronial tower 24 feet high, each side nine feet wide. Built by James Thomson of St Monans, the panels with the names of the fallen were sculpted by John Thomson of Leven, The total cost was £550, about £16,500 in current day prices. (By comparison we can note that Mr Anderson had submitted plans for houses on Bankwell Road which it was estimated would cost £800 for a 4 roomed home).[255] A "vast multitude", estimated at over 2,000 gathered for the ceremony. But absent from that number was the man whose stubbornness had caused it to be built there at all. Provost Porter had died at his home 'Bass View' on the Pittenweem Road in March 1921 aged 79.

Cellardyke's memorial had still not been built by the time the Anstruther one was dedicated. However plans were well advanced. The names to be included on the Cellardyke memorial were advertised on 27 October 1921, prompting the addition of a further 11 names to be included.

But before they could be honoured there was to be further bickering. In December 1921 a counterblast against the siting of the Cellardyke memorial on Kilrenny common was contributed to the local paper. The Common would mean the memorial was hidden out of sight. Why not build it instead, it was suggested, either at the highest point of Windmill Road or even better at the top of the Town Green? The anonymous author waxed lyrical about this latter site "the great number of the heroes whose names it would commemorate were sons of the seas" and the standing on the crest of the Town Green would satisfy "a reverent longing for just such a memorial of their dead comrades as this would be the first and last glimpse of home."

This impassioned call drew support. One sour voice seemed to suggest that there was a motive for tucking the monument way out of sight and out of mind, arguing that the Town Green was probably felt to be unsuitable as firstly it was feared that the memorial would be "wrecked by east end boys" and secondly "some noble fellow citizens who allowed other people to fight for them don't want a memorial to be placed in a prominent position as a constant reminder to them of their bravery."

Three hundred people, mostly fisherman, attended a rowdy meeting in the Town Hall. Kilrenny folk objected to the attempt to exclude the landward part of the community especially since they had contributed more per head to the memorial (22/6d compared it was said to 12/6d

---

[255] EFO 29 April 1920

from those in Cellardyke). The Kilrenny site was however dismissed as a place "surrounded by trees and whins and a bit of a swamp."[256] It was even suggested that there should be separate memorials for the landward and seaward communities.

War Memorial, Cellardyke

Relocation was *a fait accompli* and within three months it was almost completed, although the indications are that a last minute change had to be accommodated. The way in which the names of the dead are listed on memorials is telling. Some make a point of listing the most senior officer first and continuing down by rank. (So for example the Crieff memorial on which the Black Watch also predominates starts with a Captain, then two Lieutenants, ranks the 14 NCOs and finishes with 46 Privates in alphabetical order.) A feature of the First World War is that many other memorials dispense with rank altogether or at least listed the names in alphabetical rather than rank order, if ranks were given. This was taken to symbolise equality of sacrifice, representing "the idea that all those who had sacrificed their lives possessed an equality of moral achievement which transcended any other distinctions, especially

---

[256] EFO 22 December 1921

139

distinctions of class or rank."[257] In war there was a democracy of death. But sometimes military sensibilities have to be taken into account. So the Cellardyke memorial is set out with the Black Watch listed first on the Army panel staring with Private David Bell, and once all the Black Watch men were alphabetically commemorated, went on to follow suit with the Royal Scots, then the Gordon Highlanders and so on until a lone Argyll and Sutherland Highlander brought up the rear. That was until, at the last minute, even as the panels were being sculpted somebody, managed to include the name of a Corporal William Anderson of the Black Watch. Nothing is known of his service or the circumstances of his death, but had his name been submitted a few weeks earlier then by rights he would have been the first name honoured on the panel, not the last.

At long last on a dull but otherwise fine Sunday 12 March 1922 the 23 ft high monument stood above the Town Green. Depicted on it were the figures of a kilted Black Watch soldier gripping a rifle with bayonet fixed; and a sailor throwing a rope. The Burgh Coat of Arms was complemented by a plough to represent the landward area and steam drifter with the detail of a wireless fitted (as it was for patrol duty) representing the seaward. Ex-servicemen thronged the site, and were accompanied by Town and Parish councillors, members of the Boys Scouts, Girl Guides and Brownies and members of the Lodge St Ayles. The address came from Colonel TD Murray who had commanded some of the men commemorated. His speech was in large part a repeat of the somewhat idiosyncratic delivery he had made to the ex-servicemen's dinner previously. But this time he tailored it to make much of the naval tradition in Cellardyke and noted with satisfaction that by the time conscription came around, there was scarcely an able-bodied fisherman in the community who had not already volunteered for the navy. He stirred the blood by reminding the crowd that many men from the area had taken part in previous naval struggles including Trafalgar. Indeed he noted Rear Admiral Black, a lieutenant under Nelson, was the great grandfather of Cellardyke's Provost Black.

Yet although both speeches were glowingly reported neither the knight or the soldier captures for us the very personal sense of sacrifice and loss endured by those standing at the memorial without their sons (or daughter) father or brother. Far more intensely intimate and moving words could be spoken as we shall see. But at last the communities had their memorials.

---

[257] King p187

Chapter 11

The Democracy of War

War was not uniformly experienced in Anstruther and Cellardyke. For some parts of the community it meant complete dislocation of normal life. The fishing community operated under draconian restrictions which saw skippers criminalised at an unprecedented rate by being convicted and fined for transgressions. (We should not underestimate the resentment this gave rise to, as the skippers of the boats were often pillars of the community. Alex Lothian of the *Snowflight* and Henry Bett of the *Breadwinner* for instance were elders of Cellardyke Church.)[258] Crews were away en masse to the war leaving only old men and boys to man the boats and then the harbour emptied altogether as the boats were pressed into service. Despite all the fears of Zeppelin attacks and the experience by other coastal communities of bombardment the only civilian deaths locally from military action were in the fishing community, from a mine.

For other parts of the community the war was one of increasing aggravation which required adjustment but a normality could be maintained. Farming continued, shops opened, the golf club was popular, the cinema was packed. Even the voluntary efforts to raise funds for the various causes from Belgian refugees to prisoners of war were simply a realignment of normal functions - fund-raising for local causes was a regular civic activity for womenfolk and schoolchildren. As the war progressed of course the aggravation and intrusion grew greater - shortages of food, the closure of banks and post office, civic efforts to recover waste materials, and restrictions on lighting drove the effects of war deeper into daily life.

In some aspects the knowledge of the war was greater than reported in the local press. The privations of front-line life may not have been reflected in print or even in letters home but men on leave would tell their families of what it was like. And while the trenches were far away, the sea lapped up to the back doors. The Forth was a military thoroughfare and local people would have a deep knowledge of the comings and goings from the naval base at Rosyth. On September 5 1914 folk out for a walk along at Crail watching the warships manoeuvring in the Forth saw the cruiser *Pathfinder* hit by a torpedo. It took only five minutes for the British ship to sink - the first to be sunk by a German submarine

---

[258] EoFR 2 January 1913

(U21) in World War One. Two hundred and fifty men were lost in the Forth.[259]

They would also hear rumours from fishermen of submarine intrusion and of search and destroy efforts by patrol boats and destroyers. In the early days of the war the local paper felt able to speculate about one such operation on the grounds that everyone knew that something was going on, coyly recording that "there was no disguising the fact that on the sea between Anstruther and Pittenweem a torpedo boat destroyer on patrol duty fired a shot at some object in the water... a large quantity of oil was seen floating on the surface of the sea... the probabilities now point to a submarine having been sunk by the shot that was fired."[260] There was to be no more of that kind of speculative coverage as censorship was rigidly enforced. However that would not stop unrecorded local intelligence about naval operations circulating. Submarine activity in the Forth was countered vigourously. Around the Isle of May lie the wrecks of the casualties of those confrontations. On 10 March 1915 the British destroyer *HMS Ariel* rammed U-12 which sank in 55 metres of water. Another sub UB 63 was depth charged by trawlers in January 1918.[261] The enemy submarines were used to release mines and they took their toll. The steam trawler *Northumbria* was mined one mile north of the Isle of May in March 1917; the steam trawler *Columba* requisitioned by the navy was sunk by a mine on 10 March 1918. A similar fate befell the steam trawler *Emley* in April 1918. There can be little doubt that news of this activity would reach shore - indeed some of it would be heard and seen from coastal homes.

The Isle of May itself was at the hub of much activity - and there were regular comings and goings of men and supplies from Anstruther harbour. Coastguard personnel were stationed there to report on shipping movements and also on the passage of Zeppelins which used the island as a fixed point for navigation westwards. A gun battery was manned during the war and two of the Forth's motor torpedo boats were based there. Forth river pilots were also housed on the island.[262] They would have witnessed perhaps the most dramatic event of the war on the Forth - the so-called Battle of May which took place in January 1918. Although this was hushed up by the Admiralty it was an incident of which the local population can hardly have been unaware. In brief what happened

---

[259] Watson p.181

[260] CBO 5 November 1914

[261] thought to be UB 63

[262] Allan p.49

was that on the night of 31st January two flotillas of vessels left Rosyth on a massive naval exercise. Battleships, cruisers, destroyers and submarines made an impressive but barely visible 20 mile line as they steamed out with lights off and in radio silence. Such was the secrecy about the exercise however a small group of local minesweepers were operating in the Forth blithely unaware of the huge armada bearing down on them. Close to May Island confusion led to mishap and mishap to disaster. The first submarine moved to swerve past the minesweepers, as did the second but the captain of the third K14 had to take more drastic action as the little boats appeared in front of his bows. He missed them but found his helm jammed and he executed a full circle smashing into a submarine K22 which was still travelling at 19 knots. Both subs were badly damaged and lying in the water crippled, silent and dark. A battle cruiser rode straight over K22 bending the subs bow at right angles and forcing it under the water. By now there was panic stations and lights were switched on and flares fired to see what was happening. Ships turned back in an attempts to assist the stricken submarines but this only made the situation worse as the remainder of the flotilla ploughed on. *HMS Fearless* rammed K17 which sank within eight minutes. Coughing and gasping for air, 56 sailors clawed their way to the surface, only to be sucked into the propellors of the ships still passing through the midst of the mayhem. K4 was sliced almost in half by another submarine and sank with all hands. None of this information was reported in the press but it is unlikely not to have been common knowledge locally.

Late on in the war local people would have been employed in building the airfield at Crail. Three hundred tradesmen and hundreds more unskilled labourers were involved in its construction in 1918, a huge effort unreported in the press. The 27 Training Depot Squadron started operations from there in July 1918 and over the remaining months of the war local people would have seen Avro 504s, Sopwith Camels, R.E.8s. F.E.2bs and Bristol Fighters, taking off and not always safely landing. Planes lost speed, stalled, spun into the ground and sea, and within six months there had been six fatalities and as many more crash landings. The TDS with its 300 personnel was not the only unit to be based at Crail. More glamourously in August 1918 the US Army Air Corps based a detachment from the 120th Aero Squadron there, training for front line action in Avros and Sopwith aircraft.[263]

Yet in many other respects Anstruther was far removed from even home front activity. It witnessed no troop movements once the local men left

---

[263] Fife pp. 4-5.

for the front; it had little industrial activity which contributed to the war effort; there was no semblance of the industrial militancy which brought disputes in centres of population such as Perth. (Although there was a strike at Watson's oilskin factory shortly after the war.)

The biggest impact of course was through the loss of local men in the fighting. The bewildering turn of events which led to war saw the local territorials march off and fishermen sign up for the naval reserve. Men were lost steadily once these civilians got into the front-line. There was no catastrophic wipe out - the worst days of the war were when three men were lost. Certainly there were weeks when the whole district would have significantly elevated casualties but the general pattern was of isolated deaths from snipers, shellfire, and mines. This steady attrition was punctuated by violent clashes which allow the course of events to be charted through the loss of local men at key episodes in the war from Gallipoli to the Somme from Coronel to Jutland.

There is no doubt that such losses were keenly felt. From the outset of the war there was a sense that this was conflict on a different scale than had been seen before and notwithstanding the bewildering course of events which took Britain into war there was a common desire to make sense and give nobility to the sacrifice of local men. Paul Fussell has written of a raised or feudal language which was employed to designate a time of conflict and self sacrifice where a 'friend' is a 'comrade', the 'dead on the battlefield' are the 'fallen', 'obedient soldiers' are 'the brave' and so on.[264] A sense of this is evident in the elevated writing of the local press in trying to do justice to deaths in circumstances of which they knew little but which had to be portrayed as part of a cause and, wherever possible, heroic or self sacrificing. One casualty was described as having been 'wounded unto death.' This reflected the sentiments of families. The parents of George Cunningham erected a memorial stone to their son in Kilrenny graveyard on which was inscribed 'Killed while bringing in a wounded comrade at High Wood, Somme, France' amplifying the sense of self-sacrifice by adding the quotation: "Greater love hath no man than this, that a man lay down his life for his friends."

There was an apparent hierarchy of sacrifice with death in action ranking above death by accident or illness whilst in uniform, despite, or perhaps because, of the horrors of war and what must have been known about the nature of battlefield deaths. This is evidenced paradoxically by

---

[264] Fussell pp. 21-22

144

protestations to the contrary. When the local paper mourned the passing of Sergeant David Clements it stoutly argued that his death at home after being gassed was just as worthy as if he had fallen on the field "as he would have wished." The idea that soldiers would wish to die a more honourable death in action rather than in their beds seemingly persisted no matter what must have been known about the far from chivalric conflict. But perhaps there was not really a proper appreciation of the appalling circumstances of deaths which only later memoirs by old soldiers like George Coppard revealed - sniper fire splattering soldiers with the brains of colleagues that they were speaking to seconds before; men drowning in waterlogged shell holes; being trapped in No Man's Land after battle, dying agonisingly of abominable wounds or being caught on barbed wire and used for target practice by the Germans until little was left of them.

Local people wanted to acknowledge their indebtedness to those prepared to make this sacrifice long before the war had ended. A remarkably symbolic event took place in Anstruther in early 1916. Gales and a fierce snowstorm in the first week of March, had lashed the seas leaving seven corpses strewn on the shoreline from Caiplie beyond Cellardyke to as far as Billowness, west of Anstruther. Six of those appeared to be the crew of a trawler from Granton. The remaining body however remained unidentified but was evidently a naval serviceman not a fisherman. Arrangements were made to inter him locally. When his funeral took place public authorities were represented but, although he was unknown to anybody a "large concourse of the general public" also gathered. The unmistakable impression is that local people were participating in a form of the ceremonies which took place in 1920 for the interment of the unknown soldier in London and Paris, and subsequently in many other countries. It showed the felt need to honour the dead and to have them to mind.

If an unknown man could occasion such sentiment then how did the community cope with the loss of those that were known. From this distance of time and without being present on the streets when the news spread it is difficult to know. A certain reading between the lines is necessary.

In doing so it is clear that not each death had the same effect. The war did not snatch over 100 people from the streets of Anstruther leaving a void in the small community. Some of those who were lost were rarely ever seen in town - the Regular soldiers and sailors for example will have been only infrequently home on leave. Private Thomas Swan was in India for years without ever coming home; Petty Officer Frederick Blunsdon was married and living in England. The death of regular soldier Private Thomas Gilmour - the first to fall as we have established - went unnoticed. Death for a Regular far from home was an occupational hazard. But this is not to dismiss their loss as being met without genuine sympathy. Their families were present. Fred Blunsdon's father was himself an old soldier who had served for 22 years in Royal Scots including a stint of 15 years in India without a break but when he retired he came back to Anstruther. It was out of deference for him and for a family which had served its country well that his son's death was so respectfully reported.

Others on the memorial had once been familiar faces but were no longer vital members of the community although again leaving family connections behind. Emigration had been enthusiastically embraced and many of the names on the memorial are of men who had enlisted abroad in Canada and Australia, or had come back to do so. They would still be remembered by ex school friends, by ex work colleagues (such as former apprentices at Gray and Pringles.) Their parents, aunts and uncles and cousins would all mourn for them. But they did not leave a gap at a workbench or in a boat's crew.

Some have argued that the notion of a lost generation is nonsense on this count alone as emigration would have had the same effect of taking a cohort of young men out of a community to a greater extent even than the war. However I think that this is taking cold blooded calculation too far. It presumes that emigration would have continued at the same rate which may not have been the case - it would appear that locally emigration had actually peaked well before the First World War as the economic conditions in popular destinations like Canada worsened. There may not have been a net loss of people to the same extent. Secondly it is one thing for a person to be physically removed from the community by economic relocation, it is quite another to be wiped off the face of the earth. Relatives remained in contact with their far flung kin - Harry Watson remembers going to his grandmother's house and leafing through the carefully kept postcards from brothers and nephews abroad - in his case ranging from a gold miner in New Zealand to a professional golfer in Indiana, USA. They were not out-of-sight, out-of-mind but rather "the postcards spoke of a network of relations which spanned the globe."[265]

---

[265] Watson p5

Death clearly would have a greater effect on relatives than simple absence through emigration.

But many of the men would have been part of the fabric of local life. The memorial to the fallen in Elie is notable in that it provides details of the occupation of all but two of the thirty four men, alongside their name, relegating their abbreviated rank and regiment to a second row. It can be imagined how the town was denuded of familiar faces as the list includes bank clerk, builder, plumber, gardener, postman, joiner, baker and golf professional.

The Anstruther and Cellardyke memorials are more traditional and do not include such information. However we can glean details which gives us an employment profile of the casualties. As we might expect it reflects the economic predominance of the fishing industry and its ancillary trades such as coopers and ships chandlers. If we can presume that those who were lost in the RNRT were by and large fishermen (this may have been self evident as it was only rarely confirmed in local press reports) then 21 local fishermen died (one of whom was in the Black Watch). But also well represented are the landward farms and estates workers - ploughmen, farm labourers, gardeners, chauffeurs. From the town's businesses came bakers, apprentice bootmakers and printers. Gray and Pringles lost four former employees who were plumbers, ironmongers or tinsmiths; the golf club maker also saw four men killed. Then there were a smattering of professionals - clergyman, bank employee, teachers, university students.

The idea of a lost generation, it has been suggested, was not really that a cohort of young men were wiped out but rather that a particular strata within that generation had suffered grievously and disproportionately. It was perceived that the nation had lost it brightest and most gifted. The presumption was that these would be found amongst the officer class as these would largely be drawn from educated, professional cadres. What has been shown is that army officers were proportionately more likely than men to be killed and wounded giving rise to a belief that the cream of society had been swept away. Studies on casualty records have shown that whilst officers made up about 4% of the the total complement of the army, they make up on average around 6% of all deaths (based on the calculation that the British Army suffered 673,375 deaths in World War 1 of which 37,484 were officers (5.56%).[266] In a class-stratified society the officer corps was closely associated with public schools. That

---

[266] Winter p.91

147

is not to say that all officers were public school boys - but most public school old boys who joined up became officers. Foolhardy, brave, arrogant and patriotic they were cut down in swathes. 5,650 Old Etonians served, of which 1,137 were killed - almost 1 in 5, a figure which is repeated for other English public schools, leading one author to conclude that "it would seem that the products of public schools and universities were killed in rather higher proportion than officers and men from other sources."[267]

What was the experience of Anstruther and Cellardyke and indeed what would we expect it to be? Our sense of the community is prosaic, hard working, rough even with no association with the world of Wilfrid Owen, Siegfried Sassoon, Robert Graves or Vera Brittain. The officer class is depicted as being drawn from the public schools, universities and professions - not from fishermen, farmers and tradesmen. For a start, local men served and died at sea, as seamen, stokers and deckhands, out of all proportion to the national average. Only 4.6% of British deaths were in the Navy; for Anstruther and Cellardyke naval regulars and reservists constitute 25% of all the names on the two memorials.

Still, seven out of ten local men who were killed served in the Army. Of those the rank profile is as follows:

Private - 45
Lance Corporal - 7
Corporal - 3
Sergeant - 5
Lieutenant - 7
Captain - 4

Even excluding one of the officers who never served in a combat unit (but still including four privates who died either in training before going to France or back in the UK of illness not related to combat service) then the proportion of those with a commission is surprising. Fully 1 in 7 - 14% -of those locally commemorated men killed in the Army were officers. This is significantly different for the national average of Army deaths, of which less than 6% were officers. (A similar outcome is evident from looking at the Elie memorial which is almost entirely made up of Army deaths. It shows that officers comprise nearly 13% of deaths - again more than double the UK average).

---

[267] Corrigan pp57-58.

Why this should be so is difficult to know. It may be that the memorials overstate the proportion by including officers who would also be commemorated elsewhere - such as the two teachers who were both incomers, one choosing to join up with his home regiment in Lancashire. But the memorial also includes privates and NCOs with even more limited association with the town such as the Archibald brothers for example who died on the first day of the Somme. Both were born in Dollar, and had moved to the West Indies at an early age. The brothers had variously lived in Canada and Australia and seem to be included because their sister was living at the time with their aunt, a Miss Gordon, in Bankwell Road, Anstruther.

If we had a proper roll of those who served we could see whether the proportion of officers who died out of those who served was at variance with the national average. It is estimated that 15% of army officers were killed. If this was replicated in Anstruther it would mean that 72 local men would have held commissions. Although this cannot be discounted it seems unlikely. These are precisely the sort of men who before and during the war would have had a high profile in the local press. It would seem on the face of it that officers from Anstruther and Cellardyke, just like those from Eton, died in disproportionately high numbers.

The officers were not in senior ranks and were in combatant units so were perhaps even more likely to die than the average for the whole officer corps. The other thought is that these were particularly brave men who felt it was their duty to lead. John Cargill had joined up as a Private but had been promoted to Captain before going over the top to his death at Arras; Lieut. Philip Ray, had also been promoted from Private and had actively sought out action before falling to von Richthofen's squadrons guns; young Lieut. Tom Smith had sustained such severe wounds that he might have remained out of the rest of the war but after more than two years of convalescence he went back to the trenches and lost his life leading a raid on German trenches; veteran Capt. James Hay had been offered a position which would have kept him out of the frontline yet turned it down. (He too had come up through the ranks having been an NCO when in the Regular Army pre war.)

Officers like Tom Smith and Philip Ray may have been local golden boys but the grief at their passing was not because they belonged to an elite, a stratified lost generation, but because they were vibrantly local. Expressions of sorrow and dismay in the local paper were just as fulsome for Lance Corporal Willie Watson or Private George Cunningham as they were for any of the officers.

It would be natural to assume that the deaths of local men who were born and bred in the community, who worked in the staple economic activities and who would be seen in the clubs and pubs would be missed more than those who were away or were present only temporarily. And whilst the war may not have swept away a whole generation, the scale of the losses were such as to touch the whole community in a way which was not experienced even in a community which had to suffer a regular culling of its men at sea. The deaths were predominantly of course of young men, closely fitting the Scottish profile for age groups. From what we know of the ages of those who died 71.3% were under 30 years old (almost exactly the same as the 72% for Scotland as a whole.[268]) 16.2% were aged over 35 (compared to the Scottish national figure of 14%). The scale of loss meant that whole streets would be grieving for their young men at the same time. After Loos, Ian Hay the author of 'The First Hundred Thousand' said "Scotland is small enough to know all her sons by name... Big England's sorrow is national, little Scotland's is personal." If that was metaphorically true for the country it was literally the case for Anstruther and Cellardyke of course.

Tracing as best we can the names on the memorials we can establish addresses for fifty one and street names at least for another sixteen. A further eleven lived outside of town e.g. on farms and estates; eleven were not local and the addresses of fourteen are not known. Take a walk along Cellardyke today - James Street, three dead; John Street, two dead, George Street, seven dead; carry on to Shore Street, two dead and then cut up Shore Wynd and have a brief look along Dove Street - four dead from those houses alone. Walk back towards Anstruther along the streets which were built to give fisher families a better life away from the disease and squalor of the shore front homes. In East Forth Street, three dead; West Forth Street, four dead. On the next level up in Rodger Street men were lost from house numbers 1, 2, 4, 6, 10, 14 and 29. These are the bald statistics of absolute loss. Their deaths touched extended families - parents, brothers and sisters, uncles, aunts and cousins all living in the community would be affected by dread, hope, grief and despair. It does not take into account those who were wounded and broken. It does not allow for those who were lost but were not commemorated on the memorials for whatever reason.

---

[268] Lee pp. 20-21

What has to be remembered is that the memorials were a reckoning of those who were entitled to official recognition. This came by dint of being in uniform or at least in military service. This could throw up some incongruities. The list includes non combatants such as Captain George Black who had been a local councillor and baker and who had at one time been in charge of the Territorials before leaving to become commandant of a military hospital in Brighton, dying of illness at the age of 55.

It also means however that not all local men who actually died as a result of the war were included. Helen Boyter was able to ensure her 25 year old son Alex a private in the Black Watch who was killed in May 1916 was commemorated on the memorial. However her husband 55 year old Thomas Boyter, who was killed in the mine explosion which sank the *Jane* in August 1917 is not mentioned. The skipper of the boat Andrew Henderson is included presumably because he was listed as being in the Royal Naval Reserve. His sons are not.

It makes us aware that many more men died from local homes than are actually commemorated. It is not just a technicality of what qualifies as death in service as opposed to just being a casualty of war. Thirty three year old Seaman David Wilson who had left on the *Coreopsis* died whilst serving on HM Trawler *Waltham*. His parents John and Annie Wilson at 28 Shore Street mourned the loss of a second son. For David is the brother of Canadian Sergeant George Wilson whose death was so cruelly announced to his parents when their letter came back marked 'Killed in action'. Why on earth would they ensure one son's name was on the memorial but not the other?

Clearly being on the memorial was important to many families. They wanted their sacrifice to be acknowledged. Mitchell Anderson was lost from the trawler *HM Morococala*. He did not stand a chance in the frigid November waters of the Irish Sea when his boat sank six seconds after it hit a mine. It had been in the process of minesweeping, as was so often the case. His wife Euphemia ensured that he was included on both the Anstruther and Cellardyke memorials. She also had a gravestone erected in Anstruther new cemetery in his name. Furthermore he is also commemorated on the gravestone of his father-in-law (called confusingly Thomas Anderson) in Kilrenny Churchyard.

In all there are six men who are commemorated on both memorials.

Preston Hugh Keay who had emigrated to Canada perhaps typifies the sense of someone who was gone and not forgotten. The 21 year old had only recently left with his brother after serving his apprenticeship as a plumber at Gray and Pringles. His widowed mother Marjory, living at Burnside Place, clearly wanted to share her pride in her patriotic family with three sons in the forces.

Lance Corporal Hugh Keay is one of 6 men commemorated on both the Anstruther and Cellardyke memorials.

(Keay is also commemorated on his mother's gravestone after her death in 1942 aged 80).

Private Angus Mackay of the Black Watch is on both memorials. Then there is Private CM Parker who is also commemorated on his mother's gravestone. The fifth name is that of John Thomson who drowned in March 1917- he was actually buried in Anstruther so there is a grave and headstone for him in the Parish Churchyard.

Finally there is Black Watch Lance Corporal William B Watson, but to everyone Willie Watson the pigeon fancier, tennis player, bowler, churchgoer and oilskin factory worker.

Black Watch soldier advancing with fixed bayonet on Cellardyke memorial

So despite all the disputes and delays in getting the memorials built they meant much to many families of the bereaved. The two monuments which carry the message of their sacrifice are quite different in design but share fundamental characteristics. In common with many First World War memorials there is nothing triumphalist about them. The sober, stark architecture of the Anstruther monument has no figurative or decorative features. The Cellardyke memorial gives equal prominence to naval and military service. Here the figures are not shown, as in some other monuments, with heads bowed or in extremis but rather are vital and in active service. But they are not shown in any posture of victory.

Neither monuments are overtly religious. (There had been a proposal at one point to dispense with burgh memorials as the fund-raising for them clashed with the efforts to finance the local church memorials, which it was argued needed no duplication. However it was pointed out by Baillie Burd that there were Catholics and Episcopalians in the ranks of the local men who fell and there were no such churches in Anstruther).[269]

Both monuments are situated on the crest of prominent sites on either the edge of the town. This means they can be seen from the sea, as befits a fishing community. But they are not readily visible from the homes and streets. To get to them takes a special effort but although this was a criticism especially of the Billowness site it does give the locations particular resonance.

Even without religious imagery they evoke overtones of a Calvary. If people did not know why war had broken out they had a clear sense that by the end it was about securing freedom, and that men had died to preserve this for those who lived on. This is highlighted by the kinds of inscriptions which appear on local individual memorials. Take that of Coastguard JC Weir in Anstruther Parish Churchyard which seeks an acknowledgement of his sacrifice by declaring 'he suffered and died that we might live.' The monuments perched on the hill seem to suggest a similar sentiment.

Far from having the memorials situated in the middle of the town with traffic rattling by or acting as a municipal bench for the layabout, as one sceptic suspected would be the case, they are in a place of elevated solitude. People living in town even now remember a regular Sunday climb up to the Billowness memorial after church on a Sunday. The effort to pay homage to those who had made this ultimate sacrifice also suggests pilgrimage. The weekly trek was a miniature of the special trips which relatives made to the cemeteries where their men were buried or to the battlefield sites to see where they died. These were acknowledged even at the time as pilgrimages.[270]

War memorials honour the dead. They express a community gratitude for their sacrifice and it is said also to recognise an indebtedness which cannot be expunged. But the acknowledgement is not made just to the memory of the men - some of whom as we have seen may not have been all that close to or even well known to the community. It is also made to those relatives who remain behind - who are the ones experiencing loss. The memorials are not then about victory or simply historical

---

[269] EFO 4 September 1919
[270] Winter p52

acknowledgement but also, at the time of dedication, a sharing of grief. They provide a sense of belonging for the men and their families. Whether this was a real comfort we do not really know. For many of the relatives no matter how solemn the ceremony, no matter how heartfelt the gratitude, no matter the knowledge that others have suffered similarly the wonder of 'why' must have been overwhelming.

Reverend Ray
"Life can never be what it once was."

The answer to this can only come from a parent who has had to struggle with the same thought. The most knowing and affecting words of wonderment were voiced by the Reverend Ray who was asked to come back from Portobello for the dedication of the Cellardyke Church communion table. He spoke as a father not as a clergyman - he spoke in a way which expressed the permanence of sorrow; and a bewildering sense of loss.

"Every soldier we meet in the streets reminds us of them. In our dreams they rise up before us. In rooms or halls filled with people our thoughts wander to them and when the household is asleep we lie awake or sit by the fireside, thinking of them and wondering where they are."

" Life can never be what it once was. But some had to fall, my friends. That was inevitable. And why not ours."

Why not indeed? There is the sorrowful answer to every parent's cry of 'why mine'? It is the democracy of war.

Appendix 1
Brief details of those commemorated on the memorials

Anstruther Easter

Mitchell Anderson, Engineer RNR(T) (34) Killed at sea, off Queenstown Ireland when his ship *HMS Morococala* hit a mine 19 November 1917. Married to Euphemia. 2 Fowler Street Cellardyke.(Also on Cellardyke memorial)

Frederick Drury Blunsdon, Petty officer, RN (31) Killed when his submarine D5 struck a mine in the North Sea 3 November 1914. Married to Rose and lived at 164 St Augustine Rd Southsea Portsmouth·

Alex Boyter, Private Highland Light Infantry, 1 Battalion. (34) Killed when his troopship *Cameronia* was torpedoed and sunk by submarine 150 miles east of malta 15 April 1917. Worked in his father's firm Boyter & Sons in Crail Road. Lived with wife Lucy at I Melville Terrace / 2 Rustic Place.

Robert H Carmichael, Signaller Highland Light Infantry - the only RH Carmichael on record was not in the HLI but was a 24 year old private in the 9th Btn of the Cameronians (Scottish Rifles) and died on 12 May 1918. His parents lived in 24 Burns Avenue, Buckhaven, Fife.

George Moncrieff Cunningham, Private, Black Watch. (28) Killed on the Somme, shot whilst dressing the wounds of a Pittenweem soldier, 30 August 1917. Ships chandler in father's firm. (Brother Alex Cunningham, RAMC was awarded Military Medal) 'Glenogle', Crail Road, Anstruther.

George Darsie, Lieutenant, Fife and Forfar Yeomanry (35) Ex regular soldier who had served in South Africa. Emigrated to Canada. Died of wounds 31 July 1918. Son of George Darsie and Titaua Marama, a Tahitian princess, of Johnston Lodge, Hadfoot Wynd, Anstruther.

William Dunnett, Engineer, RNTS (25) Killed only a fortnight after joining his ship *S.S. "Benlawers"* (Mercantile Marine) when it hit a mine in Irish Channel 12 May 1918. Joined Merchant Navy prior to war. 6 Union Place Anstruther.

157

James Elder, Lieutenant, Black Watch (23) Reported missing, presumed dead 21 March 1918. 6 High Street, Anstruther.

James Parker Gilmour, Private, Black Watch 1 Btn, (21) A regular soldier, he was killed in action at the Battle of the Aisne 16 September 1914. This makes him the first local man killed in World War 1, yet this was never acknowledged at the time or subsequently. High Terrace, Anstruther

Francis P. Grubb, Private , Black Watch (36). Died 2 September 1916. Married to Christina Leitch Grubb, 23 Castle Street, Dumbarton.

R.C. Harrow, Private, Royal Army Service Corps, 61st Motor Transport Company. (46). Severely wounded in Arras offensive, 3 May 1917 and died 27 May 1917. Buried in Anstruther Easter Churchyard. Prior to enlisting in February 1915 was an Edinburgh Infirmary ambulance wagon driver. Brother lived at 3 Rustic Place, Anstruther.

James Henry Webster Long Hay, Captain, Seaforth Highlanders (41). Left Anstruther at age 16 after working in local solicitors office to join army. 21 years in uniform seeing service in India, Egypt and Boer war. Retired and worked for Jacob's Biscuits - re-enlisted on outbreak of war. Died 30 November 1915. Lived with wife at 21 Birchdale Road, Waterloo, Liverpool.

Elizabeth Johnston, Telephonist, Queen Mary's Army Auxiliary Corps (27). Died on Christmas Day 1918 after falling from the tower of St. Ouen Church, Rouen. Book was written about her " Johnnie of QMAAC." Brought up in the building which is now the Cellar Restaurant.

Preston Hugh Keay, Private, Canadian Engineers (21). Killed by a bullet wound through the lungs while in charge of a working party, about 8.45pm on Thursday March 16. Was apprenticed as a plumber before going to Canada with his brother. 3 brothers in the Forces. Parent's home Burnside Place, Cellardyke. (Also on Cellardyke memorial.)

H.R. Lindsay, Captain, Loyal Northern Lancashire Regiment (27). A native of Bolton, he came to Anstruther as teacher of English at Waid Academy. Awarded Military Cross in January 1916. Died at the Somme, 8 August 1916.

James Johnstone Moir Lindsay, Private, Gordon Highlanders 8/10 Btn. (25) was working at Beardmore's Works, Clydebank before joining up. Killed in Arras offensive 10 April 1917. Hadfoot Wynd, Anstruther.

Angus McKay, Private, Black Watch. (22) Killed in action 13 November 1916, mother notified in letter written by Col TD Murray of Anstruther. Had been home suffering from "trench fever" in September 1916. Lived in Kilrenny. (Also on Cellardyke memorial)

Cecil Myles Parker, Private, Black Watch 4/5 Btn (20). Previously a compositor on the East of Fife Observer. Wounded in November 1917, killed in action 3 May 1918. Union Place, Anstruther.(Also on Cellardyke memorial)

Thomas Robertson, Private, Black Watch 1/7 Btn. (32) A native of Anstruther his parents had gone to live in Leven. Died 17 June 1916.

James Smith, Sergeant, Black Watch. Had been posted missing but was known to be a prisoner of war being held at Lemberg in June 1916. Although said to be unwounded he died on 26 August 1918. Shore Street, Anstruther.

Thomas Swan, Lance Corporal, Black Watch 2nd Btn.(26) Had already served for 9 years as a regular soldier in India. Won DCM for his part in a counter attack, Nov.1914. Killed in action 5 December 1914. (Brother of William Swan) Chalmers House, Anstruther.

William Swan, Private, Labour Corps (26) Died of acute pneumonia, 29 October 1918. Buried in Anstruther Easter Churchyard. (Brother of Thomas Swan). Chalmers House, Anstruther.

John Thomson, Master Mariner RNTS (47). Prior to the war was engaged by Caledonian Ship Company, Liverpool. He was captain of liner in Admiralty service, when he drowned in an accident off Portland, Dorset, 20 March 1917. Buried Anstruther Easter Churchyard. Home was at "Rathmore" Crail Road. (Also on Cellardyke memorial)

William B Watson, Lance Corporal (24), Black Watch 1/7 Btn. Employed in his father's oilskin manufacturing business in Cellardyke. He was the first of the Anstruther Territorials to be killed in action, caught in No Man's Land digging a trench 24 April 1915. Lived with his parents at

"Craigholm", Ladywalk, Anstruther.(Also on Cellardyke memorial)

John Wilson, Private, Black Watch - died 31 October 1918. No other information known.

Anstruther Wester Memorial

James Anderson, Private, 54th Canadians (Central Ontario Regiment) (36) A mason to trade he had lived in Anstruther Wester prior to emigrating to Canada, around 1910, with his wife Maggie herself a native of Cellardyke. Killed in action 10 February 1917. (Sister-in-law Mrs Watson lived at James Street, Cellardyke)

Robert Archibald, Private, Royal Scots 16 Btn (36) Along with his brother was killed on the first day of the Somme, 1 July 1916. His father Robert Bruce Archibald went to live in Tobago after making his fortune from textiles manufacture in Scotland. After working in Canada and Australia had come to England. Pre-war lived with his wife Isabel, at 1 Trafalgar Road Twickenham (although she was staying in Edinburgh with her father the well known Scottish artist Hugh Cameron RSA, at the time of Robert's death.). His sister lived with their aunt Miss Gordon, Bankwell Road, Anstruther.

W. M. Archibald, Lance Corporal, Royal Scots 16 Btn. Killed on first day of Somme 1 July 1916 Brother of Robert (see above). Both brothers had at one time been fruitfarmers in British Columbia.

A.A. Brodie, Lance Corporal, Black Watch 9 Btn (27) Youngest son of prominent local councillor and businessman, Baillie Brodie. A golf cleek maker in his father's firm he had sought exemption from military service after conscription was introduced. Killed in action in the Third Battle of Ypres 31 July 1917.

John Cargill, Captain, Black Watch 7 Btn. A Church of Scotland clergyman he was assistant minister at Scoonie Church. A local man, he had been a pupil at Waid Academy and a graduate of St Andrews University. Joined up as a private. Died of wounds suffered in the Battle of Arras, 24 April 1917.

Hugh M. Dickson, Signaller, Black Watch 8 Btn. (24) Although learned his trade as a joiner he had been employed on a fishing drifter at the outbreak of the war. Killed in Battle of Arras, 3 May 1915. (Brother of William, killed 30.3.1918) High Street, Anstruther Wester.

William M. Dickson, Private, Black Watch 9 Btn (19) mother was informed that he had been wounded and was missing. Clung to hope that he had been taken prisoner but is recorded killed on 30 March 1918.(Brother of Hugh, killed 3.5.1918) High Street, Anstruther Wester.

Alex Doig, Private, Black Watch 4/5 Btn. Previously a coachman at Grangemuir, an estate outside Pittenweem. Joined up June 1917. Killed by shrapnel from a shell burst whilst talking to his brother-in-law 9 February 1918. His wife lived at her family home at 3 Castle Street Anstruther Wester, with their two young children.

Thomas Drummond, Private, Scots Guards 2 Btn. A locomotive fireman, he was lost in strange circumstances. He was known to be wounded on the Somme and making his way to a dressing station, but never made it and was presumed dead 15 September 1916. Subsequently his papers and photos were found on the body of a dead German. He had been recommended for a DCM prior to his death.

James Hepburn, Private, 1st London Scottish (28) Served his time in the Gas Office in Anstruther before moving to take up job in London. Killed in action 30 November 1917. High Street Anstruther Wester.

William Hogg, Private, Black Watch 8 Btn (24) Another gardener from the Grangemuir estate, he was reported missing 25 September 1915 after 3 days of fierce fighting.

Adam Lindsay, Lieutenant, Royal Scots 10 Btn. (33) a native of St Monans he was employed with the Clydesdale Bank. His wife Jeannie gave birth to their daughter on 8 April 1918; and he travelled to France the following month. He was killed on 1 August 1918. "Clifton " Pittenweem Road, Anstruther.

John Louden, Private, Black Watch 8 Btn (22). A gardener to trade he was killed in the Battle of Loos 25 September 1915, the local paper reporting gorily that his body was "caught on the barbed wire riddled with bullets". Rennyhill Cottage.

Robert Drummond Parker, Private, Black Watch 8 Btn. (20) Previously a vanman he died of his wounds 19 October 1916. (Brother of William) Shore Road, Anstruther.

William Parker, Private, London Postal Rifles (20) Had worked in Anstruther post office before moving to London. He was reported to have died of "cerbro spinal meningitis" 27 June 1915 and is buried in the City of London cemetery. (Brother of Robert) Shore Road Anstruther.

Thomas Paterson, Sergeant, King's Own Scottish Borderers (23) Another who worked on the Grangemuir estate at Pittenweem as a chauffeur to Colonel and Mrs Erskine. His family were from Kirkcaldy. Died of wounds 21 September 1917.

William Fortune Pringle, Private, Black Watch 8 Btn (22) Worked in his fathers firm, Gray and Pringle's the ironmonger from which many former apprentices and tradesmen went to war. Killed instantaneously when he was hit in the head after his battalion had taken 3 lines of German trenches during the Battle of Loos on 27 September 1915. Daisy Bank, Anstruther

George Robertson, Stoker, RN (25) Regular in Royal Navy was killed when his ship *HMS Monmouth* was sunk by the *Scharnhorst* at the Battle of Coronel off the coast of Chile, 1 November 1914. Volum Cottage Anstruther.

Alex Robb, Private, Black Watch 7 Btn. (19) A railwayman, he was killed along with William Watson on the first occasion that the local territorials reached the frontline, 24 May 1915. School Wynd Anstruther.

William Tosh, Lance Corporal, Australian Light Horse (28) He had grown up on the farm on which his late father had tenancy at Thirdpart between Anstruther and Crail. Emigrated to take up sheep farming in Australia. Killed in Gallipoli 7 August 1915. "Mansefield" Anstruther.

David Watt, Private. Black Watch 8 Btn (22) A former cooper he had survived being wounded at Loos but died of wounds suffered at battle of the Somme, 18 July 1916. A brother Tom in the Royal Naval Air service was severely wounded at Dunkirk and another, James was also killed. (see over)

James W. Watt, Sergeant, Black Watch (31) Originally a cooper in Anstruther he was transferred to the Queens Royal West Surrey Regiment after the outbreak of the war where he was a musketry instructor. Belatedly despatched to the front and was in France only 6 weeks when he was shot by a sniper 25 October 1918. His wife Thomasina lived at their home 3 Bankwell Road Anstruther.

John Cunning Weir, Warrant Officer , Coastguard Service (45) Died at City Hospital Edinburgh 14 March 1918. 24 Shore Street Anstruther. Buried Anstruther Easter churchyard.

John C. Wood, Sergeant, Seaforth Highlanders. Had also been a chauffeur at Grangemuir estate. He was wounded early in the war in the battle of the Aisne in which his brother, a sergeant major in the Cameronians, had died. Subsequently fought at Mons and the Marne before being killed 25 June 1916.

Cellardyke Memorial -

Navy

Mitchell Anderson, Engineer RNR(T) (34) Killed at sea, off Queenstown Ireland when his ship *HMS Morococala* hit a mine 19 November 1917. The boat, which had been minesweeping, sank within 6 seconds and all 13 crew were drowned. Married to Euphemia. 2 Fowler Street Cellardyke.

John Bett, Deckhand, RNRT (22) On patrol off the coast of Antrim on the R.N.R steam drifter *Coreopsis*, he was on a small boat trying to retrieve an anchor when it capsized and he was drowned, 20 April 1915. Buried at Kilrenny Parish Churchyard. 11 Shore Street, Cellardyke.

George Brown, Deckhand, RNRT . Served on H.M. Armed Fishing Smack *Ivanhoe*. Died 9 January 1919.

Alexander Brown, Deckhand, RNRT (28) died when his minesweeper, *HMMS Blackmorevale* was sunk by a mine off Montrose, on 1 May 1918. He had been with the ship for only 3 weeks, and was lost exactly 3 years to the day that he had joined up. 13 Dove Street Cellardyke.

Alexander Corstorphine, Deckhand, RNRT (19). Served his apprenticeship as a blacksmith and employed at the cleekmaking factory. Came from a fishing family (his father was the skipper/owner of the Steam Drifter *Unity*). He died after his boat *HMT Gambri,* was sunk by a mine off the Royal Sovereign Light Vessel, 18 January 1918. Buried in Kilrenny Parish Churchyard. "St. Abbs" West Forth Street, Cellardyke.

James Muir Gourlay, Deckhand, RNRT (23). On active service on *HMS Western Queen* in North Sea when he contracted influenza which became pneumonia. His family had received a letter saying that he had been very ill but he had got over the worst of it; followed by a telegram the next day that he was dangerously ill. He died with his parents by his side in Ingham Hospital, 15 July 1918. Interred in Kilrenny with naval honours attended by his 4 brothers all in naval service. 6 Dove Street, Cellardyke.

Andrew Henderson (Jnr), Skipper RNRT (53) Was not on active service but was fishing off St Abbs Head in his motor yawl *Jane* when his crew pulled in the nets which contained a mine on 14 August 1917. The explosion also cost the lives of his two sons Alexander(29) and Andrew (27), as well as two other crew members James Wilson and Thomas Boyter. None of them are commemorated on the memorial. 38 West Forth Street Cellardyke.

Alexander C. Keay, Mate, RNRT (25) Another young fisherman to lose his life whilst minesweeping, when *HM Trawler Repro* was sunk off Tod head. 26 April 1917. 29 Rodger Street, Cellardyke.

William Tarvit, Trimmer, RNRT (22) Information about the Tarvits who served and died is confused. However as William died at home his death certificate is available. He was a cleek finisher in a local factory, and may have been discharged with shock from service aboard the Gunner *Pelagos* prior to his death from consumption on 13 October 1918. He died at the family home at 2 Harbourhead, with his fisherman father James, (who was also on active service on the Motorlaunch *Granton*) at his bedside.

Robert Thomson, Leading Seaman, RNR (35) Served on *HMS Armadale Castle*, and survived the war only to fall victim to the flu epidemic which swept the nation, and military forces, dying at Plymouth Naval Hospital, 17 October 1918. George Street.

Robert Watson, Mate, RNRT - no information

Alexander Watson, Skipper, RNRT (50) Attached to *HMS Vivid*, died 30 May 1919. Buried in Kilrenny Parish Churchyard. 50 John Street, Cellardyke.

David Watson, Deckhand, RNRT (43) His boat, the steam trawler *Aster*, hit a mine in the Mediterranean in July 1917. David died 13 October 1917. Born in Cellardyke but lived with his wife at Torry in Kincardineshire.

John Christie, 2nd Engineer, RNR (25) having served on the cruiser *HMS Monitor*, he was transferred to the trawler section and lost his life when *HMPMS Queen of the North* hit a mine off Orfordness 20 July 1917. The Queen of the North was a 22 year old paddle steamer which prior to the war ran day trips from Blackpool to Douglas on the Isle of Man. 29 men were lost in total when it sank. 4 George Street, Cellardyke.

James Dick, Seaman, RNR (21) yet another lost to a mine when *HM Trawler Evadne* sunk off Owers Light Vessel 27 February 1917. (Brother of Andrew Dick - also on memorial) 14 East Forth Street.

Robert Gardner, Seaman, RNR (22) was said to be the first from Cellardyke to go on naval duty, serving firstly on a transport vessel and then as a gunner on *S.S Greynog* which was sunk when torpedoed without warning by a submarine on 18 April 1918. 2 Rodger Street, Cellardyke.

James Anstruther Moncrieff, Stoker, RNR (22) A fisherman he had been an engineer on the local trawler *Vanguard III*. He served on *HMS Invincible* in the battle of the Falklands when the British ships sunk the *Scharnhorst*. Was lost when the *Invincible* was sunk at the battle of Jutland, 31 April 1916. "St. Helens", West Forth Street, Cellardyke.

William Reekie, Seaman, RNR (22) Lost when *HMS Clan Macnaughton* foundered in the North Atlantic 3 February 1915. His ship was an armed merchant cruiser and was not thought to have been sunk by enemy action but lost either to the heavy weather or because of structural problems caused by the addition of armaments and plating.

Robert Thomson, Leading Seaman, RNR (35) Had been home on leave for a month from his ship *HMS Armadale Castle* for the first time in 16 months in April 1918, but subsequently died 17 October 1918. Buried at Kilrenny Parish Churchyard. George Street.

William Watson, Stoker, RNR. Although in the Royal Navy he fought as a soldier with the Royal Naval Division Hood Battalion and was killed at Gallipoli, 4 June 1915.

John Morris Wood, Seaman, RNR (23). Served as a gunner on *S.S. Wellaston.* Died 8 January 1919. Buried Kilrenny Parish Churchyard. 26 Fowler Street, Cellardyke.

John Thomson, Master Mariner RNTS (47). Prior to the war was engaged by Caledonian Ship Company, Liverpool. He was captain of a liner in Admiralty service, when he drowned in an accident off Portland, Dorset, 20 March 1917. Buried Anstruther Easter Churchyard. (Also on Anstruther memorial.) Home was at "Rathmore" Crail Road.

Army

David Bell, Private, Black Watch (41) An army regular he had 20 years of service behind him including having fought in the Boer War. Was wounded at La Chappele on the Western Front before being killed in Mesopotamia. Left behind 5 children aged between 12 and 2. " Frithfield" Anstruther.

Alexander Bissett, Private, Black Watch 1/6 Btn. (21) A baker, he was killed by a shot to the head, 22 July 1918. His father a cabinet maker with Gray and Pringle was sent postcards recovered from his son's body, looking forward to the end of the war.

Alexander Boyter (Brown) Private, Black Watch 7 Btn (25). Served apprenticeship as a plumber with Gray and Pringle although he had been a stoker on a drifter immediately prior to the war. Was killed by a shell burst on 31 May 1916. His late father (not on memorial), was a fisherman who had been killed by a German mine in the North Sea. 1 Rodger Street.

Alexander Smith Boyter (Smith) Black Watch 6 Btn (24). In civil life was a spinner at Messr Watson and Cos Roperie. Seriously wounded in eye in the early engagements of the war, and sent home to recover. Back at the front he was badly burned; and then survived a trench collapse when sandbags fell on him, as a result of which one of his comrades was instantly killed and another had his back broken. Killed by shrapnel coming through window of building in which he was sheltering, 16 September 1917. 5 George Street, Cellardyke.

Alexander Boyter (Bowman) Private Black Watch 8 Btn. (22) A plasterer to trade he was killed in a bombing raid on German trenches 19 October 1916. 14 Rodger Street Cellardyke.

George Corstorphine, Private, Black Watch 8 Btn (25) A ploughman before joining up he had recovered after being wounded at Loos. Shrapnel wounds to his neck saw him brought to England for treatment but he died at Orpington hospital 10 August 1917. Buried in Kilrenny Parish Churchyard. 28 West Forth Street, Cellardyke.

Andrew Dick, Private, Black Watch 6 Btn (19) Joined up under age when the war began and on active service for 3 years. Twice wounded and gassed once which saw him brought to Elie Hospital to convalesce. Killed 6 weeks after returning to France, 10 April 1918. (Brother of James, also on memorial.) 14 East Forth Street.

John Doig, Private, Black Watch 7 Btn. (20) was training with the rest of the East Neuk territorials at camp in Kinghorn when suffered "an unexpected weakness." Died at his father's home 10 Dove Street on 20 November 1915. Buried in Kilrenny Parish churchyard.

Angus McKay, Private, Black Watch. (22) Killed in action 13 November 1916, Mother notified in letter written by Col TD Murray of Anstruther. Had been home suffering from "trench fever" in September 1916. Lived in Kilrenny. (also on Anstruther Easter memorial).

Cecil Myles Parker, Private, Black Watch 4/5 Btn (20). Previously a compositor on the East of Fife Observer. Wounded in November 1917, killed in action 3 May 1918. Union Place, Anstruther (also on Anstruther Easter memorial).

Robert Shirreff, Private, Black Watch 8 Btn. (20) Another of the golf cleekmakers, he was a machine gunner when he was posted wounded and missing in action. No further news was heard of him and was presumed killed 19 October 1916. 59 George Street, Cellardyke.

William B Watson, Lance Corporal, Black Watch 1/7 Btn. Employed in his father's oilskin manufacturing business in Cellardyke. He was the first of the Anstruther Territorials to be killed in action, caught in No Man's Land digging a trench 24 April 1915. Lived with his parents at "Craigholm", Ladywalk, Anstruther. (also on Anstruther Easter memorial)

Alexander Watson, Private, Black Watch (20) An apprentice printer, he was shot in the head by a sniper whilst in a frontline trench on 22 November 1916. Lived at home with his widowed mother Agnes at 58 James Street, Cellardyke.

Robert Watson, Private, Black Watch 1/7 Btn. An apprentice plumber, he was with the local contingent of Territorials at Kinghorn camp when he "contracted a chill whilst on manoeuvres" and died in the family home 17 James Street, Cellardyke on 19 April 1915. Buried Kilrenny Parish Churchyard.

Charles Elder, Corporal, Royal Scots. As late as January 1919 his parents placed an advert in the local press appealing to returning POWs for information on their son who was reported missing 12 April 1918 (and presumed dead on that date.) East Pitcorthie, Anstruther.

William Moncrieff, Private, Royal Scots (35) Lived with his wife Annie at 7 Gordon Street Leith. He survived the appalling train crash at Gretna in which many of his Edinburgh Royal Scots had been killed. Killed in Gallipoli 28 May 1915. Parent's home Shore Street, Cellardyke.

Thomas Smith, 2nd Lieutenant, Royal Scots (21) A student at St Andrews University, he was wounded in the chest by shrapnel in 1916 only a month after leaving for the front. Brought back to hospital in Aberdeen to recover and returned to frontline in April 1918. Was posted missing and possibly taken prisoner after leading a raid on German trenches 16 May 1918 - but later presumed killed on that date. 6 Rodger Street Cellardyke.

John Smith, Private, Royal Scots. Killed by a sniper's bullet as he was withdrawing from the frontline on 28 December 1916. Previously employed in the cleekmaking factory. 10 Rodger Street, Cellardyke.

Andrew Halcrow, Private, Gordon Highlanders (27) Previously a cooper with Wolkholf and Co. in Aberdeen. Killed at Arras, 9 April 1917. Home was at 22 John Street, Cellardyke where he lived with his wife Isabella.

Wallace Low, Private, Gordon Highlanders (19) Was an apprentice bootmaker with his father in the shop in James Street but joined the Cameronians when he reached military age. Killed on the Aisne, 25 July 1918. East Forth Street.

George Moncrieff, Private, Gordon Highlanders (20) had been a baker in George Birrell's shop in George Street. On 3 August 1918 he was in an advanced position in front of the British trenches when a shell splinter killed him. (Brother of John - also on memorial) 16 George Street, Cellardyke.

John Herd, Private, Canadian Infantry 3rd Btn. (Central Ontario Regiment) (19). A machinist, he was born in Anstruther although his family appear to have emigrated as his mother was living at 148 Christie Street Toronto when he was killed on 8 September 1917.

Alex Moncrieff, Private serving with the Canadian Infantry (Alberta Regiment) 31st Btn (33) a cooper to trade, he was killed 5 May 1916. (Brother of William - also on memorial.)

George Wilson, Sergeant, Canadian Infantry 31st Btn.(Alberta Regt.) (26) had served his apprenticeship as plumber/ tinsmith with Gray and Pringle's before emigrating to Canada in 1913. News of his death only received by his parents when a letter was returned to them marked " Killed in action. Location unknown." 28 Shore Street, Cellardyke .

Andrew Carnegie Black, Sapper, Royal Engineers (23) had been a miner in the west Fife coalfields. he was caught by an enemy mine explosion 20 February 1916. Lived with Margaret, his wife of only 4 months, at 62 James Street, Cellardyke.

David Allan Clement, Sergeant, Royal Engineers Reserve Coy, (20) Joined up with the Fife & Forfar Yeomanry but transferred to the Royal Engineers to get to the front more quickly. Was gassed and sent home to recuperate, but suddenly died at his parents farm at East Pitkerie, Anstruther, on 19 March 1917. Buried in Kilrenny Parish Churchyard.

George Black, Captain, ROF (55) A local baker and Councillor, he had at one time been the commanding officer of the Anstruther Black Watch

Territorials was sent to become the commandant of a military hospital in Brighton. Died of illness, 29 June 1918.

James Cairns, Lieutenant, RASC (28) Had emigrated to become a farmer in Australia returning to join up in 1915. Attached to the London Regiment, posted missing believed killed 23 April 1918. (Brother of WL Cairns - also on memorial). Son of the laird, James Lindsay Cairns of Mount Stuart, Elie.

W.L.Cairns, Gunner, Canadian Royal Artillery (25) like his brother James had emigrated but in this case to become a farmer in Saskatchewan. Killed 6 September 1917.

P.H.Keay, Canadian Engineers (21). Killed by a bullet wound through the lungs while in charge of a working party, about 8.45pm on Thursday night March 16 1916. Was apprenticed as a plumber before going to Canada with his brother. 3 brothers in the Forces. Parent's home - Burnside Place, Cellardyke. (also on Anstruther Easter memorial).

John Moncrieff, Lance Corporal, Seaforth Highlanders (28) Had served his apprenticeship with the Cellardyke firm of Melville and Co. and then moved to South Shields for work. Killed on the first day of the Somme 1 July 1916. (Brother George - also on the memorial) 16 George Street, Cellardyke.

James Murray, Corporal, Canadian Highlanders 15th Btn.(Central Ontario Regt.) (21) Born in Cellardyke. Employed as a clerk in Canada. Killed at Ypres on 22 April 1915. 4 Rodger Street, Cellardyke.

Philip Oliphant Ray, 2nd Lieutenant, Royal Flying Corps (23) Son of the former minister of Cellardyke Parish Church, joined the Cameronians from Glasgow University where he was studying engineering. Commissioned as 2nd Lieutenant in the 8 Btn Black Watch. Joined RFC and was shot down at Arras on 13 April 1917 by Baron von Richthofen's squadron. The Manse, Toll Road, Cellardyke.

David Robertson, Private, Scots Guards, - no information.

Andrew Robertson, Private, Labour Corps - no information

Robert Paterson Smith, Lieutenant, Machine Gun Company, Seaforth Highlanders 8 Btn. (29) Came to Cellardyke as assistant headmaster in February 1914 and was interim headmaster till March 1915. He was attached at first to the Royal Scots. Killed 2 August 1918. A native of Newtongrange.

John Thomson, Lance Corporal, Argyll and Sutherland Highlanders 7 Btn. (20) Had been employed in Clydesdale Bank Anstruther. In April 1918 admitted to hospital, wounded in thigh by shell splinter. Septic poisoning forced amputation. He recovered from the operation sufficiently to write to his parents but died 9 June 1918. 22 James Street, Cellardyke

William Anderson, Corporal, Black Watch - no information.

Note on sources

Much of the information on the fate of local men is drawn from the pages of the local newspapers. There were two papers, owned by rival members of the Russell family. The senior title was the *East of Fife Record* which had been published for more than 50 years by the time of the outbreak of war. By contrast the *Coast Burghs Observer* was only launched in 1914. However it outlasted its better established cousin. The *Record* was a commercial casualty of the war. Its editor George Black Russell was commissioned into the Royal Scots in April 1915. By 1917 the paper's workforce had been reduced to only five compared to a pre-war staff of twenty two. There was also the small matter of the financial strain caused by having to pay for a libel action arising from a pre-war story in which the paper had unwisely claimed that a popular beverage of the time was made out of horse flesh. The paper closed in August 1917. The remaining title became the *East Fife Observer.*

Specific additional information has also been provided by descendants of some of the servicemen.

The information was cross referenced where possible with the Commonwealth War Graves Commission. Where there is a difference such as age or address I have tended to use the information from the local paper on the assumption that those inserting an intimation in the paper are more likely to know where they live or their son's age than the authorities.

Bibliography

Alexander, Jack, *McCrae's Battalion: the Story of the 16th Royal Scots* (Edinburgh, 2003)

Allan, James, *The Isle of May* (Anstruther, 2000)

Anderson, Agnes, *Johnnie of Q.M.A.A.C.*(London, no date)

Baird, Bob, *Shipwrecks of the Forth* (Glasgow,1993)

Bennett, G., *Coronel and the Falklands* (London, 1962)

Bishop, Alan and Bostridge, Mark (eds.), *Letters from a Lost Generation* (London, 1999)

British Vessels Lost at sea 1914 -1918 (Cambridge, 1979)

Brown, Malcolm, *Tommy Goes to War* (Stroud, 1999)

Brown, Callum G., 'Piety, gender and war' in MacDonald and McFarland (eds.) *Scotland and the Great War*

Chamier, J.A., *The Birth of the Royal Air Force* (London, 1943)

Clark, Alan, *The Donkeys* (London, 1993)

Condell, Diana and Jean Liddiard, *Working for Victory 1914-1918* (London, 1987)

Coppard, George, *With a Machine Gun to Cambrai* (London, 1999)

Corrigan, Gordon, *Mud, Blood and Poppycock* (London, 2003)

DeGroot, Gerard J., *Blighty - British society in the Era of the Great war* (London 1996)

Dennis, Peter, *The Territorial Army 1906-1940* (Suffolk,1987)

Dixon,W. MacNeile, *The Fleets behind the Fleet* (London, no date)

Dorling H. Taprell, *Swept Channels: Minesweepers in the Great War* (London, 1938)

Douglas, Sholto, *Years of Combat Vol I* (London ,1963)

Eunson, Eric, *Old Anstruther* (Ochiltree, 1997)

Fife, Malcolm, *Crail and Dunino - the story of two Scottish airfields* (Peterborough, 2003)

Falls, Cyril, *The Life of a Regiment. The History of the Gordon Highlanders Vol IV 1914-1919* (Aberdeen,1958)

Ferguson, Niall, *The Pity of War* (London,1999)

Franks, Norman, Giblin, Hal and McRery, Nigel, *Under the Guns of the Red Baron* (London, 2000)

Fussell, Paul, *The Great War and Modern Memory* (Oxford, 2000)

Graves, Robert, *Goodbye to All That* (London,1960)

Grieves, Keith, *The politics of manpower, 1914-18* (Manchester,1988)

Halpern, Paul G., *A Naval History of World War 1* (London,1994)

Harding, Bill, *On Flows the Tay - Perth and the First World War* (Dunfermline, 2000)

Hay, Ian *The First Hundred Thousand* (Edinburgh and London, 1916)

Haythornthwaite, Philip, *The World War One Source Book* (London,1994)

Holmes, Richard, *Tommy - The British Soldier on the Western Front 1914-1918* (London 2004)

Hough, Richard, *The Great War at Sea 1914-1918* (Oxford, 1983)

Hugh, Cecil and Liddle, Peter (eds.) *Facing Armageddon: the First World War Experienced* (London,1996)

James, Robert Rhodes, *Gallipoli* (London,1965)

Jones, D.T., Duncan, J., Conacher, H.M., and Scott,W.R., *Rural Scotland during the War* (London, 1926)

Jones, H.A., *The War in the Air Vol III* (Oxford, 1931)

Keegan, John, *The First World War* (London, 1999)

King, Alex, *Memorials of the Great War in Britain* (Oxford, 1998)

Liddle, Peter,(ed) *Home Fires and Foreign Fields* (London, 1985)

Liddle, Peter, *The 1916 Battle of the Somme* (London, 1992)

MacDonald, Catriona, and McFarland E.W. (eds.) *Scotland and the Great War* (East Linton,1999)

MacDonald, Catriona, 'Race riot and representations of war' in MacDonald, and McFarland (eds.) *Scotland and the Great War*

MacDougall, Ian, *Voices from War* (Edinburgh, 1995)

MacEachern, Dugald, *The Sword of the North. Highland Memories of the Great War* (Inverness, 1923)

Merewether, Lt. Col. J.W.M., and Sir F.Smith, *The Indian Corps in France* (London, 1918)

Middlebrook, Martin, *The First Day on the Somme* (London,1971)

Moore. J (ed) *Jane's Fighting Ships of World War 1* (London, 1990)

Mosier, John, *The Myth of the Great War* (New York, 2001)

Ogilvie, D.D. *The Fife and Forfar Yeomanry 1914-1919* (London, 1921)

Petre, F. Lorraine, and Wilfrid Ewart, and Major General Sir Cecil Lowther, *The Scots Guards in the Great War 1914 - 1918* (London, 1925)

Reeves, Nicholas, 'Through the Eye of the Camera: Contemporary cinema audiences and their 'experience' of war in the film 'Battle of the Somme.' in Cecil and Liddle (eds.) *Facing Armageddon*

Robb, George, *British Culture and the First World War* (Basingstoke, 2002)

Royle, Trevor, *The Flowers of the Forest- Scotland and the First World War* (Edinburgh, 2006)

Smith, Peter, *The Lammas Drave and the Winter Herrin'- A history of the herring fishing from East Fife* (Edinburgh, 1985)

Smout, T.C., *Nature Contested* (Edinburgh, 2000)

Spiers, E 'The Scottish soldier at war' in Cecil and Liddle (eds.) *Facing Armageddon*

Stevenson, Stephanie, *Anstruther* (Edinburgh, 1989)

Sym, Colonel John, *Seaforth Highlanders* (Aldershot, 1962)

Taylor, A.J.P., *English History 1914-1945* (Oxford, 1965)

van Emden, Richard, *Boy Soldiers of the Great War* (London, 2005)

Vansittart, Peter, *Voices from the Great War* (London, 1998)

Watson, Harry, D., *Kilrenny and Cellardyke* (Edinburgh, 1986)

Winter, Denis, *Deaths Men* (London, 1979)

Winter, J.M., *The Great War and British People* (Macmillan, 1985)

Winter, J.M., *Sites of Memory, Sites of Mourning: the Great War in European Cultural History* (Cambridge, 1995)

Winter, Jay, and Sivan,Emmanuel, *War and Remembrance in the Twentieth Century* (Cambridge, 2000)

Young, Derek, *Forgotten Scottish Voices from the Great War* (Stroud, 2005)